BY EDWARD FIELD

Stand Up, Friend, with Me (1963)
Variety Photoplays (1967)
Eskimo Songs and Stories (1973)
A Full Heart (1977)
Stars in My Eyes (1978)
New and Selected Poems (1987)
Counting Myself Lucky: Selected Poems 1963–1992 (1992)

ANTHOLOGIES

A Geography of Poets (1979)
A New Geography of Poets (1992)
    (with Gerald Locklin and Charles Stetler)

EDWARD FIELD

COUNTING MYSELF LUCKY

SELECTED POEMS 1963-1992

BLACK
SPARROW
PRESS
SANTA ROSA
1992

ACKNOWLEDGMENTS

Some of the previously uncollected poems have been published in *AKA Poetry, American Poetry Review, Am Here Forum, Bay Windows, The Cafe Review, Calapooya Collage, Chiron Review, 5 A.M., Colorado Review, Exquisite Corpse, Free Lunch, Gathering of Poets, Genre, Grand Street, Jewish Frontier, Mid-Coaster, Michigan Quarterly Review, Movieworks, The Nation, The New Republic, Off the Page* (Video), *OutWeek, Pearl, Poetry Now, Redstart, Telescope,* and *Western Humanities Review.*

Black Sparrow Press books are printed on acid-free paper.

LIBRARY OF CONGRESS CATALOGING-IN-PUBLICATION DATA

Field, Edward, 1924-
   [Poems. Selections]
   Counting myself lucky : selected poems, 1963-1992 / Edward Field.
     p.   cm.
   ISBN 0-87685-890-6 : $12.50. — ISBN 0-87685-891-4 (hard) $25.00.
— ISBN 0-87685-892-2 (ltd.) : $30.00
   I. Title.
PS3556.I37C68   1992
811'.54—dc20
                                 92-32538
                                 CIP

AUTHOR'S PREFACE

When I discovered the poetry of Cavafy—almost immediately after I began writing—I recognized at once that this was my master. Oddly, on the ouija board Jack London later presented himself as my "guiding spirit," but he seemed highly irritated with me, so I don't think he will mind me introducing this selection of a lifetime's work by invoking the spirit of Cavafy, who wrote, "The true artist does not have to choose between virtue and vice, but both will serve him and he will love both equally."

I myself wouldn't use the word "vice"—it's just me I'm writing about. But my poems do tell a lot of my secrets, and I can't help it—this is after all from the book of my life. Writing for me is such a private act that when I see my poems in print, they embarrass me, like the dream of being the only one naked in a crowd. My poems expose me to the world. And they're so easy to understand, which makes it all the more embarrassing, as if some part of me, too, wished to observe the rules of polite discourse. How I envy poets who keep buttoned up! But as Cavafy said, that has nothing to do with poetry.

For me, writing has always been a means of self-exploration, but beyond that, I see poetry as a mysterious force. Perhaps it's not meant to save the world, but maybe, if we are very true to its spirit, it can influence things in some way for the better, help a few people, at least—much as the 23rd Psalm has healing powers and has often rescued me.

TABLE OF CONTENTS

NEW POEMS

The Winners and the Losers

Confessions of a Hypochondriac

Bio

Shark Island

Evening, with Leaves

SELECTED POEMS

from STAND UP, FRIEND, WITH ME (1963)

from VARIETY PHOTOPLAYS (1967)

COUNTING MYSELF LUCKY:
SELECTED POEMS 1963–1992

THE WINNERS AND THE LOSERS

GANESH

How lucky to be born with an elephant's head,
and have those flapping ears, and laughing lips,
but best of all, a trunk
to curl around the leg
of anyone you didn't want to leave.
I'd smile with my little round elephant eyes
and sit on your lap—everyone
would want me to sit on their laps.
And you know what they say
about the size of the nose?
You'd all have the fun
of feeling me up
to see if it's true what it shows.

THE WINNERS AND THE LOSERS

I stood before them
and told them of my life,
the sorrows and the losses —
in short, the human condition.

I could see them all, so young,
hair shiny, with their lives before them —
they were looking on me as a loser,

and had no pity,
so determined were they
to make it big, to be winners.

Even the clerk in the social security office
looked at me with wonder and asked:
Have you always earned so little?

I had never thought of it that way —
to her too I was a loser
with bad luck written all over my tax records.

What happened to the beautiful losers of my youth
who let the world destroy them
but stayed true to their dream,

scoffed at materialism, conventions,
a small, beleagured band
who kept their integrity against the world
and devoted their lives
to Art, Sex, and Revolution?

Youth once believed in them,
the madmen who burned themselves out with drugs and drink,

disappeared into the desert
or battered society with their shaggy heads.

There was one period even
when everybody was rushing off
in search of the underground man.

But now that winners are in fashion,
disappearing are the last of the bohemians
left over from the old days of the Village,

and I am of another era, like the grizzled poet
who slept in Village doorways
and showed up at the Poetry Society
with his life work in a shopping bag

and read his poem "Crows":
Caw, caw, he cried, as he jumped
off a table, flapping his arms.

THE DOG SITTERS

for Stanley and Jane

Old friends, we tried so hard
to take care of your dogs.
We petted them, talked to them, even slept with them,
and followed all your instructions
about feeding and care—
but they were inconsolable.
The longer you were gone
the more they pined for you.
We were poor substitutes,
almost worse than nothing.

Until you returned, days of worry
as each fell ill with fever, diarrhoea and despair,
moving about all night restlessly on the bed we shared.
We wakened at dawn to walk them,
but there was a mess already on the rug.
We called the vet, coaxed them to eat,
tried to distract them
from the terrible sadness in their eyes
every time they lay down with their chins in their paws
in utter hopelessness, and the puppy
got manic, biting our hands.

Ten days in the house by the bay
trying to keep them alive, it was a nightmare,
for they were afraid to go anywhere with us, for fear
you would never come back,
that they must be there waiting when you did,
until you did . . . if you did. . . .

Then, the minute you got home
they turned away from us to you

20

and barely looked at us again, even when we left—
for you had filled the terrible empty
space that only you could fill,
and our desperate attempts
were dismissed without a thought.

We tried to tell each other it was a victory
keeping them alive, but the truth is
that when someone belongs so utterly to someone else,
stay out of it—that kind of love is a steamroller
and if you get in the way, even to help,
you can only get flattened.

WAITING FOR THE COMMUNISTS

after Cavafy's "Waiting for the Barbarians"

What's all the commotion about?
I haven't seen the city in such an upheaval
since the last power failure.

     Haven't you heard? The communists are coming today.

Is that why so many people are packed into the stadium,
watching the giant television screens?

     Yes, everyone wants to see what the communists look like.
     Listen to them roaring for blood.

Why is Congress passing laws one after another
and the President, for once, not vetoing them
but signing them furiously?

     Oh, they're making one more attempt to ban the
        communists.
     But it won't do any good—when the communists get here
     they'll make their own laws.

Why are government emissaries rushing to the harbor, the airport,
carrying pink frosted cakes and party favors and hats?

     Because that's the kind of junk they say communists like—
     they're just barbarians, you know.

Why are the rich driving right behind them,
their wives in furs, arms and throats glittering with diamonds,
their cars loaded with opulent gifts—gold bars,
deeds to real estate, country club memberships?

Because the communists are coming today
and they want to buy them off. They hope their elegant
    wives
will soften a little the hard hearts of the communists.

Why are the supreme court justices putting on their robes
and taking their places gravely on the bench?

    Because after the government flees to its fortified island,
    the judges will have to sign the surrender.

So why don't our big shots stand up now and make their
        speeches,
warn against the communists like they're always doing,
tell us how we must sacrifice, remain vigilant,
to protect our homes, our way of life?

    Because the communists are finally coming
    and nobody wants to listen to that stuff anymore.

But why this outbreak of muttering in the crowds?
(How serious everyone looks, how confused—even angry.)
See how the streets and squares are rapidly emptying,
and everybody going home so deep in thought.

    Because it's evening and the communists haven't come.
    And some people just back from abroad say
    there aren't any communists anymore, maybe never were.

Oh my God, no communists? Now what's going to happen?
You've got to admit they were the perfect solution.

MINOR VARIATIONS

1.

Navigator to Pilot: Help,
I'm being attacked
by the Y'Know Virus.

Pilot to Navigator: Blast it
with the virus-killer missiles.

Navigator: No use,
there's, y'know, a swarm of them.
Everytime, y'know, I shoot one down, y'know,
another one, y'know, gets through.

Pilot: Y'know, we've already gone through invasions
of Like, Sort of, I Mean, Kind of Thing
and Really,
but where the hell
did this one, y'know, come from,
outer space?

Navigator: Y'know, if I knew that,
maybe they wouldn't, y'know,
be driving me,
I mean, sort of, like, really, y'know,
crazy.

2.

There once was an insect who said,
y'know, y'know, y'know.

Soon all the others were also
saying y'know,
every other word,
it was such fun,
until that's all they said:
y'know, y'know, y'know.

And that's why they're called
Crickets.

WHATEVER BECAME OF: FREUD?

Has the age of psychology really passed?
Aren't people interested anymore
in how toilet training shaped them?
Nowadays, nobody talks of their "analysis," or even
the less respectable therapies that came into fashion
about the time we gave up on the couch —
encounter groups, group gropes, group games, and finally
just lying on the floor, screaming out the pain.
Or even, on the lowest level
(which we all descended to in desperation),
self-help books: How to Overcome Depression,
Get More Confidence, Be Popular.

But usually, we were safely in the hands of Freud,
whose theories, a whole generation beyond Marx swore,
would rescue mankind from its lot,
and even, in the views of Reich, end war
when we liberated our sexuality
by working through the body's armouring
to release our soft and loving primal selves —
war and love supposedly being incompatible —
also by sitting for hours in the orgone box to absorb
the sexual energy of the universe.

Those were the years when we were all convinced
we were "neurotic," discussed our neuroses passionately,
analyzed our dreams with friends over coffee
and endless cigarettes — we were fiendish smokers —
talked of breakthroughs, insights, and sometimes with awe
of "graduation," when the "neurosis"
would finally be "cured," which meant
you had worked through your blocks, your inhibitions,
and were no longer Acting Out Negative,

but had found your niche in society—
marriage, a career, and forgiving your parents—
and worried whether this meant the end of creativity.

The air is clearer since "phallic symbol"
has gone the way of "penis envy" and "Freudian slip."
Nobody nowadays blames their failures on their neuroses,
and if you say "transferences," everyone assumes
you're talking about your bank accounts.
It's no longer news the discovery
(and Freud deserved the Nobel Prize for it)
that people's minds are always on sex.

But with the same obsession we had with Freud,
and the same narcissism (how we beat each other
with that faded cry), people nowadays are able to simply
turn away from "problems" and wallow in their pleasures,
making a cult of health, often devoting themselves
just to working on their bodies. Did I say "just"?
Even Freud was always looking for the roots
of neurosis in the body. And as Claudette Colbert said
on observing Marilyn Monroe's buns,
"I would have had to start at thirteen."

Sadly, true. For us old devotees of the therapies,
the cornerstone of our faith, You can change your history,
proved to be bad Freud, and even worse, a fraud—
far more expensive than the gym. Years of talk,
and nothing got solved. Except the language of it
seemed to define the losses of a generation,
and for all its radiant promises, that was all.

THE ROMANCE OF EXTINCT BIRDS: THE CARRIER PIGEON

These talented and plucky creatures
said to have been wiped out in World War I
by the gunfire of both sides,
carried vital messages infallibly home.

They weren't like most pigeons
for whom corn and screwing make up the good life.
If you were a spy behind enemy lines,
you always had one of them tucked up your sleeve,

and when you got some vital dope
you fastened the coded message in a capsule
on the pigeon's leg, and sent it
winging home innocently across the lines.

What valiant work they did, these birds,
often getting shot, but flying on
to deliver their messages with the last wingbeat,
blood staining the commander's palm

as he felt the tiny fervent heart go still,
and the eye clouded over.
But it wasn't just gunfire that did it:
the wireless was invented,

that war ended—
some creatures need to be needed or they die—
and the carrier pigeons vanished,
the feathered heroes.

BLINKS

"When you wind up a Helen Keller doll what does it do?"
"It walks into the wall."
All blind jokes are anti-blind,
but it's true you've got to watch them like a hawk —
I look away for barely a second
and there he is going off in a crazy direction.
He could get killed like that,
but there's an angel looking after them.

He used to hold onto my shoulder on the street,
but doesn't like the image that gives him
(being blind doesn't make him less of a WASP),
so I am forced to steer him by his shoulder.
He likes that. I get taken for the blink.

A man holding another man's shoulder
doesn't raise an eyebrow in Italy,
or in the Moslem world where men walk hand in hand
and if a man meets a friend and his wife,
shakes hands with the woman and kisses the man.
Even in England it's okay, the way we walk,
because everyone is too polite to notice.
Or in Holland where no man would touch another in public,
no one would dream of making a remark.
Only in the States are we in danger,
where everything between men
is interpreted as sexual.
A goodhearted truckdriver, stopping for a red light,
leaned out of his cab and shouted,
"Hey, watch out! AIDS!"
As if a hand on a shoulder could transmit the virus,
or perhaps he was nervous
one thing would lead to another.

But it's not always goodhearted, the attention.
To protect us from fag bashers I suggested
he carry his fold-up cane open so no one could miss it,
but this too would give him the wrong image.
Now, passing groups of kids I half-close my eyes
as if I were the blink, like a woman I know,
coming home on dark streets,
acts crazy to deter muggers and rapers.
If we start having real trouble,
I'll have to wear dark glasses and carry the cane.

Here's one that's not only anti-blind, but anti-guide dog:
A woman saw a guide dog leading a blind man
right into the moving traffic to cross the street.
Getting to the other side, she was astonished to see
the man feeding the dog a biscuit. "Excuse me, sir," she said,
"why are you rewarding that dog? Don't you know he nearly
got you killed?" "Sure," replied the blind man,
"but I have to find out where his mouth is,
so I can kick his ass."

As if foreshadowing his fate,
in childhood he invented a game with his sister:
Push the Blind Man into the Traffic.
Now he both hates the cane as the symbol
of his difference, and rages against the sighted,
saying he'd like to strike out with it right and left,
just as I'd like to poke it into the wheels of bicycles
that whizz by and miss us by a hair.
He mutters again and again the words
of his mobility instructor at the blind school,
who taught him to negotiate the streets with a cane—
the world isn't set up for the blind.

Curious how the folded-up cane in his hand,
is stared at by black people
who take it for magic juju sticks or a weapon,
something for power.
Customs officials examine it as if its hollow shaft

was full of drugs, and one of them once asked
if it was karate sticks. Latinos
sometimes take it for a traffic warden's baton
and ask directions, which he, an old New Yorker,
is perfectly able to give,
just as he can figure out where we are in London,
from the time when he could still see.

He'd like being blind to be classier
and imagines a Broadway musical, Blinks on Parade,
with a row of chorus boys in high-style mirrored sunglasses,
tapping their white canes back and forth to a jazzy beat,
though frequently it turns into a sci-fi/horror film,
called Revenge of the Blinks.

According to how they feel about the blind, people,
he claims, are either HB or AB.
Horror of the Blind is understandable.
Who wants to have to think about such a calamity,
and most people, hurrying on their way, resent
having to help a blind man at the curb,
helplessly banging his cane to be crossed.
They so often have off-putting blindisms
like rocking in place or grinning insanely.

It's a relief to joke about it,
but the one about *the blind man passing a fish shop,*
manages to combine anti-blind and anti-woman sentiments:
> *He tilted his hat, and called out with a friendly grin,*
> *"Good morning, ladies."*

The other half of the race, he says, suffers
from AB, Adoration of the Blind.
Black people are the most afflicted
with this special sympathy, he says, even dope dealers
will stop dealing and see that he gets safely by
a broken sidewalk, an obstacle, even those
who resent whites will help him—perhaps because

they are people with soul, and besides, they know
blinks have to be color blind.

Italians always try to sit them down,
though there's nothing wrong with their legs.
In fact, sitting down and eating
is what makes fatties of too many, though feeding them
is at least something you can do.
The world ignores the problems they have getting laid,
and for a long time, the books pushed on them
were spiritual works, perhaps to get their minds
off their horniness. Take it from me,
dirty books is what they want, if not sex clubs
and hustler services, to make it easier:
another blink I know hands out his card in the subway,
counting on his handicap for getting away with it,
though he's slightly defective besides.

In my role of guide I have to help daily
with a million little things—finding a slipper,
unjamming the tape player, spreading peanut butter,
combing his hair. You have to be prepared for a crash,
and yelling, Don't Move!, race to sweep up the shattered glass.
How powerful, clever, useful and virtuous,
that makes me feel, with my eyes
that solve so many problems, and then furious
when he isn't grateful, or when he doesn't
catch on to something I'm explaining, the dumb blink—
perfectly simple, with eyes—or offended
when he lets me have it for telling him what to do.
He particularly resents
my taking his finger and trying to guide it
to the right button on the tape player, for instance.
He always gives it to me for moving things
so he can't find them, and it's even my fault,
when he walks into me, for being in the way.
But then, I nearly give him a heart attack
if I speak when he thinks I'm out of the room.

They have a perfect right to hate us,
but somebody has to tell him
when it's a curb or wheelchair ramp,
or when there's a hole or dogshit on the sidewalk,
or a head-level metal sign or low-hanging branch,
or a little dog or child he might step on.
"Veer left," I'm always saying, and it annoys him
to take orders, because it's his nature
to be the one in charge, or he complains
when I warn him too late, his foot
already in the air over the precipice.
Luckily he has a strong back—
mine would have been in a brace long ago.

Even if I sound disenchanted, half-agreeing
with those who say, "Shit,
better put them out of their fucking misery,"
or sometimes muttering "I'd kill myself if I was blind,"
I've got an incurable case of AB,
for as a sighted guide, I found,
after lonely years of near-suicidal misery,
my role in life—helper,
or as I sometimes feel, slave.
It's a lot of work, full time without a break,
if you're thinking of going for it, baby,
and unlike seeing-eye dogs, who are sent
to a farm in the country when they get old and tired,
I'll probably drop dead in harness.

ROACH INVASION

1.

I'm just dozing off,
    when a roach crawls over me—
that makes it New York already.

A roach on a bald head
    leaves . . . footprints? pawprints?—anyway,
there's no dropping off again,
    with the roach tracks tingling.

You swat yourself about the head,
    then reach over to turn on the light
to look for the dead roach on the pillow
    or cagily hiding under the pillow,

turn off the light,
    get up to pee,
lie there worrying about your aging prostate.

It is then the mind begins to race
    as you despair over your career,
everything stacked against you,
    age, out-of-style, enemies.

Now you're thinking of the refrigerator,
    the crackers,

turning on a bed of nails,
    the next day already ruined.

34

2.

While I'm
preparing
dinner
the baby
roaches
come,

but prema-
turely meet
their fate
beneath
my thumb.

3.

The roach population of New York
has survived aerosol sprays, Roach Motels
where "they check in and don't check out,"
and now even the vaunted
sure-fire killer Combat.

Boric acid they skip through lightly
as the first snowfall of winter.

At the end of my rope, I cry to Heaven,
do you expect me to live with this, or what?
Sign up with a Buddhist guru
who teaches making peace with all God's creatures?

What do animal liberation activists say
about the roach's rights?
But what about mine?
Who pays the rent around here anyway?

BERLIN '87

*"Berlin is a monster, though one
before which we must have the
greatest respect.*
— Minna Bernays to Sigmund Freud

1.

It is not what it is, but where it is
that makes it fascinating.
For this is the most sensitive border in the world,
yet one possible to cross—for us to cross—
with less red tape than foreigners face
coming into our own country—
a miracle considering the paraphernalia of hostility here,
like walls, minefields, tank traps, and armies
on both sides.

At the checkpoint, photographers
cluster, waiting for another daring escape.
Someone stands hour after hour,
holding a poster, appealing
for the release from communism's clutches
of a sister, a husband, a son.
Tourists climb a platform
to view across the ominous gap the streets
where a woman, not trying to escape or screaming for help,
wheels a baby carriage, and workers are restoring
long-neglected, bombed-out buildings.
The tourists find looking across
more thrilling than just going there.

Our side: the Showcase of the West, fat as a pussycat,
claws retracted but teeth sharp and gleaming.
Over there: more somber, the grandiose imperial center,

36

with better food for the money, cheaper transportation,
and do I only imagine the people are nicer?
Or is it that I've been brainwashed
to expect them to be soulless monsters
and it's a welcome surprise if they're human at all?
Or has a harder life made them better,
and it's capitalism that brings out the worst in people?
An unthreatening populace there,
even if they are dying to travel west, but can't.

A busload of American soldiers
rides through the checkpoint for a day's visit.
They talk of bargains, buying shoes.
Mysteriously, a car barely stops for showing papers—
an ambassador, perhaps—
everything is of heightened significance.
But the old trudge over to our side freely
to return home evenings with full shopping bags.
We others have to wait in lines for visas,
ten minutes or half an hour. The first time
in that drab shed with unmarked doors you tremble,
remembering a lifetime of movies, news stories, novels,
where they are the bad guys and we the good—still,
there *are* the watchtowers with spotlights, armed guards.

Then, the dramatic moment
when visa in hand you walk across no-man's-land,
and with an *auf wiedersehen* to an official,
you push through a simple gate and are there.
Across the Iron Curtain. In East Berlin.
So simple, you want to gasp. Then remember, *for us.*
You are in those very streets
glimpsed from the viewing platform. You stare at everyone
as if they lived on the moon, read posters,
check window displays, prices, walk on, trying to take it in
that people are living ordinary lives here,
and the baby carriage contains
not a uniform that will get you to freedom, but a baby.
You are unprepared for the baby. It is only

when you sit down in a restaurant and eat
that normality returns a little,
and the iron curtain built across your mind
comes down forever.

2.

Forty years ago, I bombed this city—"Pinpoint bombing"
meant five thousand bombers dropping their loads
within a square mile. Yet life went on for them
almost normally to the end, and it is surprising
how much remains—a city so solid, we got only the tops
and rubble-heaps of decorative stonework—
though there's a large, empty plain now
conveniently between the two halves.
But out of the remnants, the fragments, my mind
keeps reconstructing the Bismarkian capital
in all its baroque splendor, its bombastic proportions.
And overlaying that, the Berlin of the Nazis
with uniforms, swastikas, flags, roundups and torture chambers.
Both seen through the scrim of the modern, divided city—
almost bland, but never boring—
and still the locus of high drama.

The restored Reichstag is now a historical museum,
and in a remote room a corner is devoted
to the murder of the Jews,
just one event in German history, we are reminded—
the figure 4,500,000 is printed on the wall,
the lowest possible number
quoted by those historians who don't deny it altogether—
as if that minimizes anything. There is a curious
lack of courage in owning up,
and not much evidence of guilt, outside a few memorials
in corners of the city. Across from the opulent
KDW department store where fur-clad matrons flock
is an underground station built National Socialist style,
a monument to the heroic, patriotic dead—it needs no plaque,

the message is in the granite and the brass.
Outside on the square, a simple metal sign
listing the names of the death camps
"that we may never forget." So much expense and feeling
in the granite memorial for the storm troopers,
so flimsy the one for the Jews.

At least East Berlin has left standing in remembrance
the ruins of a synagogue burned on Kristallnacht,
plants growing from crevices in the shattered stonework.
West Berlin has a bombed-out church, but gradually
has transformed it into an art object
with an elegant neon clock, modern glass enclosure below,
the stonework shored, the rough edges smoothed,
like a bejeweled dowager who has raised hell too often
but is going to obscure it with jewels and glitter.
They cannot bear to leave anything messy. In the Tiergarten
an overgrown field bears the sign: "This field
has purposely been left wild
to show what the heath was like in its natural state"—
in case citizens should take the authorities to task
for the disturbing disorder.

Down the block from where I'm staying, a plaque appears:
"Christopher Isherwood lived here from 1929 to 1933,
and wrote . . ." et cetera. 'Thirty-three, the ominous final date.
So many dates end in the Thirties, tombstones
in the Jewish cemetery engraved euphemistically,
"Died in the East." No bodies could be in those graves.
Suddenly the wall is comforting,
for in spite of the smart clothes worn on the Ku'damm
you hear the uniform tramping of the shoppers' feet
and sense the passion for order,
the devotion to social regulations
followed to the letter.

No matter how we are drawn back to Germany and the Germans,
as long as the wall remains, the length of the divided land,
we all sleep better.

TIJUANA BLUES

Now that the Berlin Wall is down,
that we cried shame about for years,
how about our own wall, that we maintain
with the same display of righteousness—
On one side Us, the rich and powerful,
on the other the hungry, Them.

Driving down from San Diego to Tijuana,
crossing the border is not too different
from Checkpoint Charlie—for them,
there are our border patrols,
dumping them back, as often as they sneak over,
into the land of their desperation.

But we go over at will,
like we used to in Berlin,
to walk around in wonder.
And like in Berlin, there's a difference in the people:
on our side, a particularly American blend
of smugness, arrogance, ignorance.
On the other, Spanish-Indian soulfulness,
gentleness, and grace.

We leave Avenida Revolucion, garish for tourists,
and walk around the Mexican town where the shabby stores
and even the cathedral lack the opulence of . . .
I almost said the West, when I meant Yankeeland.
East Berlin, of the Second World, was incomparably
grander, cleaner, and the food was better.
Tijuana is of the Third,
a city hooked to a border,
its barriers, like the wall in Berlin, bristling

with all the military devices money can buy,
but which with persistence can be jumped.

When we were treated well by the East German guards,
our German friends said, "They don't treat us like that.
It's only because you're Americans."
Here, in Mexico, why are people so kind to us,
I wonder, when they face such a wall of insult?
They should be full of hate, but instead
answer our phrasebook Spanish softly,
melting our hearts.

On our way back to the border crossing,
beggars lie in wait:
a little man sprawls on the ground blowing a tune
on a blade of grass between his thumbs—
all he has to make music with,
and boys strum toy guitars and sing like little caballeros,
irresistibly off key, while equally little mothers
offer gimcracks for sale. We empty our pockets
of our last pesos before escaping through the gate.

In San Diego, the Latinos working
in garages and restaurants seem grateful
for any attention if your eyes
merely recognize them as human,
something that perhaps doesn't happen very often.
These are the people I want to know, I think,
but after work, they're whisked off to a somewhere else
that draws the line between us.

San Diegans just ignore them,
attempting to wipe out of mind
what they fear is a human tidal wave
poised on the border.
It would be a major improvement if it broke,
and worth what it cost, as in Germany
with the wall down—nothing to pity the Germans for,
they begged for it for years.

Our wall keeps growing higher, and more expensive,
but no one protests. The injustice
of two centuries is now fixed
in electronics, in concrete, in cold hearts,
as we refuse to share the land and its riches
we took away from them,
proclaiming it ours.

DIETRICH

She never had to make up
for not being popular at school—
she started out well beyond all that.

She was never a bobbysoxer, for example,
nor one of those girls fighting
against going all the way—
you don't go from that to where she is.

When she sings "My ideal is a big blond man"
or "Every night another bliss"
you know just what she means by this.

Ancient in Paris,
perfect setting for monuments
where the boulevards culminate
in a granite bust,

where the populace adores
the will that invents
an inviolable mask—
still she writes "This rotten world,"

as if tied to a mast and forced
to witness, as she always has—
her eyes windows
with the shades permanently up.

HEAR, O ISRAEL

At age sixty-four, waking in the night
not with a hard on, alas, but indigestion,
I, son of Jews from the shtetls of Poland and Russia,
of a father with the eagle profile of a sheik
and a mother with a goyish nose,
give my testimony for the Moslem world,
maligned as fanatic and backward, even evil.

What a privilege to have been to Morocco,
where people are robed like in the Bible,
and over the high Atlas to the Sahara,
the beginning of the silk route to Asia . . .
and Tunisia with desert roads that end
in salt flats or an oasis, that's the chance
you take, if you are a traveller . . .
and to have breathed in the dust of Cairo,
the germ depository of the Nile . . .
and holy Jerusalem, built over a spiritual fault
that can never allow peace, but heightens the spirit . . .
and beyond, the long overland route to Afghanistan on a bus,
with intimations of the Gobi Desert and China in the nostrils. . . .

My God, how much I've learned in that world,
not least, that I was a man—
those Wise Ones, they look in your eyes and see what you're
            worth,
and I don't mean in camels or Cadillacs—though baksheesh,
a gift, is never amiss.
Still, they are the ones who always give gifts,
making one's soul flower in gratitude.

That world that feeds the soul taught me
that I was a man and had a soul, and if mine
is a tormented one, at least it experienced itself fully
on the journey through the desert, squatting
in the slender shadow of a palm tree, of a broken-down bus,
or among oleanders with robed men,
drinking mint tea bees hover over.

It is a world where, unlike ours, men like each other,
where, looking deep into your eyes,
men are not afraid to take your hand
and say, Come stranger, break thy journey and linger awhile
so that we may open our lives, our hearts to each other,
before we move on refreshed. . . .

How many times have I lugged my valise
through the turmoil of peddlers at the bus depot
down a dusty road, past shops and hovels closed up
in the midday heat, past long walls
that shut you out absolutely, revealing only
white domes against a blue sky
and a minaret with loudspeakers
for the recorded muezzin call at prayer times,
or sometimes even a white-clad figure on the high balcony,
chanting to the four corners of the town
for all to come and pray—
a long, weary trek.

Any voyage there begins at dawn and lasts all day,
but after dust and thirst, you might arrive
at green palm groves criss-crossed with rivulets,
and at the heart, a blue pool
where holy beggars are washing themselves
and someone is always doing his laundry.
There is somehow a hotel nearby
or at least a teashop to come out of the sun, a melon
to share, and coarse desert bread one could live on.
It is of its essence
that after you go beyond despair,

lugging that damn suitcase in the sun,
plagued by beggars and flies,
surrounded only by desolation, poverty and waste,
and are ready to give up,
this world can transform itself
from a garbage dump into a garden,
enveloping you in attar of roses.

On my floors are rugs I have brought back,
a bit of . . . The Mysterious East.
Here, where so much is phony, the wool retains
something of the caravan, the nomad flocks,
that makes cats go crazy on it.
Woven into the patterns with bits of straw and dung
are fragments of a forgotten language, glimmers
of meaning . . . about ancestry, about honor, memories
of our history even, that special strand
reminding me what Jew means:
one who remembers, one who has it woven
into his being to remember.

Tonight, with the Shema—Hear, O Israel—on his lips,
let this old Jew give his tribute to the Moslem world,
that has preserved our connections to ourselves,
to the old times, that can remind us
what we have lost, that can still
teach us who we were, who we are.

Hear me, Israel, before the insanity of the world,
the lack of love for our brothers,
leads to the destruction of us all.

I seal this testimony with a kiss
to my soul's beloved, my sacred brother, as we embrace
with beating hearts in the long night.

SONG: *TROP TARD POUR PARIS*

Returning to France after years
I can only feel regret
for a life I never lived.
Too late now, I say,
trop tard pour Paris.

But maybe a part of me didn't leave
in the long ago of my youth
when, broke, I signed on the freighter home,
but stayed behind as a kind of ghost
to live a parallel life to mine.

Here, in the so-familiar Parisian air
is still the suspicion of a ghostly me,
skinny as ever, unchangeably stubborn and young,
who never got on that boat, and unlike me,
didn't need any money or a job to stay.

And while I lived out my New York life
—analysts, transient loves, the years—
my Other went on floating through the chill mists
of the city he could never bear to leave,
the only place he could ever feel at home.

And yet, by giving up Paris, I gained
the rest of the world, it's true, though I know
it's here I should have lived my life.
Now it's too late, too late for me,
trop tard pour Paris.

CONFESSIONS OF A HYPOCHONDRIAC

"Listen, they're still dying
of all the old things, too."
—Sam Menashe

THE HYPOCHONDRIAC

Obsession with health can easily take over
from sex as life's major problem,
though sex feeds it like kindling,
for isn't that moist and warm intimacy
the perfect vehicle of transmission,
the kind doctors say there's no cure for
and, a little voice whispers, the explanation
of half your ailments, not to say the penalty
for having the soul and habits of a whore?

It's the perfect solution, a way of life,
filling in chinks of time like smoking or cruising,
until it becomes the major mental activity
and especially a torment in the night,
as you enumerate your symptoms over and over
to a doctor who never existed, a Miracle of Sympathy
willing to take complete care of you,
saying everything's all right, saying it
so you believe him and assuring you
your symptoms aren't serious. . . .

But I'm not reassured, I'm furious.
He's implying, isn't he, that it's all my imagination
when I know something's surely there
and if looked into more thoroughly could be found?
On the other hand, I don't want anything
to be found—once defined
it would be hard to live with, and scary
to have to defy Medical Authorities
who want to put me on drugs with Side Effects—
I have an ineradicable suspicion
that all drugs have to be poison.

And if I admit my symptoms aren't yet dangerous—
after all, I'm still walking around and nothing shows—
an even worse torment to endure is
I'm convinced that before it's too late
I could be cured.

NEW YORKERS

Everywhere else in the country, if someone asks,
How are you? you are required to answer,
like a phrase book, Fine, and you?

Only in New York can you say, Not so good, or even,
Rotten, and launch into your miseries and symptoms,
then yawn and look bored when they interrupt
to go into the usual endless detail about their own.

Nodding mechanically, you look at your watch.
Look, angel, I've got to run, I'm late for my . . . uh . . .
uh . . . analyst. But let's definitely
get together soon.

In just as sincere a voice as yours,
they come back with, Definitely!
and both of you know what that means,
Never.

After a lifetime insisting
that all my problems were psychological/sexual
or political/economical, according to
whichever Great Thinker I was reading,

hypochondria has forced me to pay attention to my body,
the body I've always accused of betraying me,
treated as an enemy, and hated
for not being what in others I admire.

Now it's up to me to try to get to know it at last,
release it from its adjustments to old fears
that mis-shaped it, and misused for years,
threatens breakdown at any time.

Indeed, how have I survived this long,
ignorant of what I do —
my body is as unconscious as my mind.
Of course, others I see are in worse shape,

victim to all the illnesses on the obituary page.
Don't look at others, the wise man said.
First, know thyself: You have mortal weaknesses.
It's probably too late to do anything about that,

but even so everything must be changed.
Letting the tensions in the body go
is almost impossible at this point, though —
or does that "almost" nurture a tiny hope?

No, it's pure terror that drives me,
no matter how tired, to study myself in the mirror
that tells me what I'm doing wrong or right —
warding disaster off for one more night.

The Centaur

Look, below he's a horse
on proud haunches cantering.
Above, a lithe rider, Lord of the Air.

From glossy rump to shock of hair,
that's the way a man is meant to be —
if life hasn't crushed him, as it has me.

My rider is poorly seated, out of rhythm,
holding on with a cruel bit
to the slack, bony beast below with broken gait.

How badly I have treated him,
and do it yet.

A Doggerel of Symptoms

Physicians and doctors,
        I'm down on my knees.
I beg you to listen,
        my symptoms are these:

To begin at the top,
for several years
I've had a buzzing in my ears
which doesn't stop
but switches its irritating note
from low to high and back to low,
and related to it somehow
there's a clicking like a cricket
in the ear tube that's connected
to a permanent sore spot in my throat.

Doctor, it isn't a cold,
        don't tell me to endure it,
that it's simply part of growing old—
        I'm asking you to cure it.

The stiffness in my neck's become
a permanent condition—
in bed, it's hard to find
a bearable position.
And one of my armpits stings
like a maddened killer bee.
What's worse, it's on the heart side.
That doesn't worry you? It worries me—
as well as the way my chin
gets itchy in the night.
I dreamt it was pinworms,
but even if that's not exactly right,

it could still be an amoeba
or another parasite.

You say, though, there's nothing wrong,
        that it's all imagination?
But I know what I feel and can describe
        in detail each sensation:

I suffer from electric leg,
and muscle cramps in bed —
a warning that sciatica,
a word I speak with dread,
is about to clamp its yellow
teeth on me again,
drive in its railroad spike —
my God, sciatica's a pain
no other pain is like.

Another anxiety is my tongue.
I know it's too much to expect it to be
as pink and smooth as when you're young,
but lately it's alarmingly fissured
and stays a little sore —
that has to be significant, but doctors don't
look at the tongue anymore —
it's out of fashion, so they won't.
Yet, since I bit it at the end
it's lazy, clumsy, numb.
Not only is it hard to speak
(the consonants don't come)
but it's dangerous to eat a steak
the way I like it, red —
I can't distinguish meat from tongue
and chew myself instead.
I read a ghastly book when I was young
with vivid illustrations of
the ailments of the tongue.

Try not to worry, it's all in your head,
    you Freudian doctors say.
Yes, but if only reciting the symptoms
    would make them go away.

My fingernails are growing in
with ridges, cracks and bumps,
and the bottoms of both feet
are crapulous with lumps.
And even though I floss and brush
everytime I eat,
I'm permanently afflicted with
receding, pitted gums.

And that special burning in my groin,
could it be a tear?
A venereal virus settling in,
causing a rupture there?
I've more than a slight suspicion
it's from sexual indiscretion—
and pain when I pee
keeps reminding me
the urethra's a perfect ladder
for viruses to climb into the bladder,
a mucous breeding ground in fact,
making sex, indeed, a risky act.

I'm scared as I unzip my jeans
    to see the drop that might be pus.
Please tell me, doctor, what it means,
    and if it's really serious.

There's always something I've forgot—
an ache, an itch, a darkening spot,
asshole often a little sore
(more often sore than not),
and in kidneys, liver, guts, and heart
flashes of pain like a semaphore,
warnings dangerous to ignore—

and other things I can hardly stand
to mention, like my prostate gland—
though no strange rashes yet,
no diarrhoea, no waking in a sweat,
just nervous tics, arthritic knees
painful, hard to bend—

There! I've told my symptoms from the start,
but dreading the name of my disease,
can never get quite to the end.

Something I'll admit,
        I'm not ashamed of recognizing it:
                okay, I'm a hypochondriac.
Then why can't doctors also
        admit they do not know,
                instead of blaming everything on my
                        being such a nervous wreck,
and when they do, why can't I
        just get up and go,
                instead of writing out the check?

Up Shit Creek in a Heatwave

First, the air conditioner started dripping,
not outside like it's supposed to, but inside,
and for days I was in despair as I wrung out
towels sopping from the window sill,
until the solution occurred to me—
bang it on the bottom with a stick.

That problem solved, immediately, the kitchen drainpipe,
corroded with age, started to leak
just when the building employees went on strike,
and for days, it seems, I was emptying
pails of sludge from under the sink.

This too was, in time, repaired,
but I began to sense a cosmic pattern in it,
the universe on a roll of dripping and leaking,
with one leak plugged, another breaking out,
and nothing, ultimately, to be done.

But wait, today my wail of informed despair
was stopped when the faucet
turned and turned and the water
didn't come on, reversing the trend
from leaking to blockage, as if something cosmic
had answered my prayers.

But now, trembling, I have to ask:
What the hell does all this mean
in relation to my prostate?

PROMISES, PROMISES

Leaving aside the drinkers and dopers
whose lifelong obsession has its own trajectory —
weak proselytizers, though they keep urging
us to join them in a drink or a toke,

many invite us to follow,
promising miracles of mind and body.

Whatever you do, you've got to die
of one thing or another,
but terrified, you've also got to try
one thing or another.

Still, the gurus and the devotees,
isn't it their fate, like ours,
to die from some disease,
and with age deteriorate?
Or do people who do yoga all their lives
die peacefully in the lotus posture
rather than, like most of us, from cancer in the ward?
And busy with chopping, shredding, blending, and juicing,
do vegetarians, fruitarians, and fasters
live healthy till they die,
in spite of looking gaunt and terrible?

Is there really any way to avoid doctors and disease,
or is it all crackpot theories?

People who eat in coffee shops
are not worried about nutrition.
They order the toasted cheese sandwiches blithely,
followed by chocolate egg creams and plaster of paris
wedges of lemon meringue pie.
They don't have parental, dental, or medical figures hovering
full of warnings, or whip out dental floss immediately.
They can live in furnished rooms and whenever they want
go out and eat glazed donuts along with innumerable coffees,
dousing their cigarettes in sloppy saucers.

Aunt Edwina's Five-Minute Blender Recipes

Dollinck, with my schedule
if it takes more than an hour, it's out.
Better five minutes.

Like for borscht. The Old Country way
takes about three days, right? Mine's instant:
dump acana beets inta da blenda
with juice of a lemon and container of yoghurt,
and turn it on—that's all.
If you're sluggish in the bowels
you'll have such a crap,
you'll feel like putting on your sequinned sunglasses
and going to the track.

Too fat? Do yourself a favor and make my gazpacho:
into the blender go whole tomatoes,
green pepper, cucumber and onion,
a clove garlic, lemon juice, and olive oil—
soy sauce if salt's not out.
Serve it with chopped-up cucumber
and you won't notice the bits of skin or seeds.
Eat nothing but, and you'll get so skinny
everybody will be after your ass—
but use a condom, pul-ease.
Also great for shitting—all real food is.

Better than a trip to the Middle East,
and safer these days, eat my hummus.
Throw half a can of chick peas in,
with some of the liquid, a garlic clove, lemon juice,
and once they're blended, a few tablespoons tahini.
It's thick, so stop the blender once or twice and stir.

If this doesn't put lead in your pencil,
nothing will—don't expect food
to be more than part of the solution.

"I HAVE ALWAYS SAID THAT IF I GOT IT"

I have always said that if I got it
I wouldn't go to a doctor who'd treat it
with surgery and chemotherapy as if it was caused
by something outside, an invading enemy,
but to a quack, who'd see it as part
of the body's functioning — my own body
doing this to itself, me doing it.

But right now, the main thing I need is reassurance,
and with the authority of its procedures,
the medical profession is reassuring
that all possible is being done,
and even if it doesn't succeed, at least done thoroughly.
With quacks, it seems insubstantial,
almost trivial before mortal danger,
unless as a terminal case with nothing to lose
you go in for wheat grass, diets, or faith healing —
they also work sometimes, I guess.

Of course, I can talk
because my body hasn't broken down yet —
it just isn't working very well these days,
and intimations of disaster flood me
as weird little symptoms break out.

This is me, I have to remind myself.
The body, the cancer, and all,
it's mine
and I mustn't let them take it away,
cut it, bomb it, or burn it. . . .

But oh, to have such nerve
and defy the whole medical establishment. . . .

My God, why this terror?
What am I in the grip of?
Is it mere death that terrifies me so?

"SOME SAY THE BODY CURES ITSELF"

Some say the body cures itself
and that the symptoms I so fear
are its way of self-healing
like the fever it fights infection with.
And if the body is curing itself, they say
to let it, don't interfere
even if the process feels funny and scary—
it knows how to, better than any doctor.
And you have to remind yourself over and over
it's all being taken care of.

(It might also be true
that nature's clearing the decks
by getting rid of you.)

BOMBA THE JUNGLE BOY IN "FANGS OF DEATH"

He was always escaping on a vine
across the pit of snakes —
green mambas, cottonmouths, corals, and vipers,
whose bite meant instant death.

His pursuers arranged diabolically for the vine to break
so of course he fell in, but then moved
with incredible softness among the coiled automatons,
not to alarm them.

That boy cannot fail, we know, even though we
are so in terror watching him we don't dare breathe,
but he breathes, beautifully —
you can't move like that if you don't.

Immunologists say that for every invader
the body can produce a specific defence,
or as a Christian Science pamphlet put it,
even in a shark-filled sea, do not despair, something,

a porpoise, maybe, will come and guide you,
the world is perfect, and disaster
nothing but lack of faith
which puts you outside of that perfection.

But I do believe there can be no error, Lord,
and everything is getting into balance all the time,
even plagues, wars, tidal waves, slaughters —
all part of the law, your necessary work.

And as you saved that boy from the fangs of death,
protect me now, fallen

from tightrope into snakepit among your glittering cobras
spread heads poised to strike.

O help! Help! Help me
accept the life and death of it, go on breathing,
and in the depths of my jungle being exult in it,
as the whole exploding cosmos does.

Physician, Heal Thyself

The rabbis say Choose life
All I can say is I'm stuck with it
so okay then I choose

They whisper there is no error
in the universe
be of good cheer

For the moment then I have contempt
for my death Let it terrify me again
tomorrow in the night

All I can do is do my yoga daily
say my prayers live till I die
and let what takes me take me

BIO

THE LAST BOHEMIANS

for Rosetta Reitz

We meet in a cheap diner and I think, God,
the continuity, I mean, imagine
our still being here together
from the old days of the Village
when you had the bookshop on Greenwich Avenue
and Jimmy Baldwin and Jimmy Merrill used to drop in.
Toying with your gooey chicken, you remind me
how disappointed I was with you for moving
to Eighth Street and adding gifts and art cards,
but little magazines, you explain, couldn't pay the rent.
Don't apologize, I want to say, it was forty years ago!

Neither of us, without clinging to our old apartments,
could pay Village rents nowadays,
where nobody comes "to be an artist" anymore.
Living marginally still, we are shabby as ever,
though shabby was attractive on us once—those years
when the latest Williams or Stevens or Moore was sold
in maybe five bookstores, and the Horton
biography of Hart Crane an impossible find.
Continuity! We're still talking of our problems
with writing, finding a publisher,
as though that were the most important thing in the world—
sweetheart, we are as out of it as old lefties.

Someone came into my apartment recently and exclaimed,
"Why, it's bohemian!" as if she had discovered the last
of a near-extinct breed. Lady, I wanted to protest,
I don't have clamshell ashtrays, or chianti bottles
encrusted with candle wax, or Wilhelm Reich,
Henry Miller and D. H. Lawrence,
much less Kahlil Gibran and Havelock Ellis,

on my bricks-and-boards bookshelves.
But it's not just the Salvation Army junk she saw,
or the mattress and pillows on the floor—
my living style represented for her the aesthetic
of an earlier generation, the economics, even,
of a time, our time, Rosetta, before she was born.

The youth still come weekends, though not to "see
a drag show," or "bull daggers fighting in the gutters,"
or to "pick up a queer or artist's model."
But there is something expectant in them
for something supposed to be here, once called,
(shiver) bohemian. Now it's I who shiver
as I pass them, fearing their rage against
an old guy with the sad face of a loser.
Daytime, it's safer, with couples in from the suburbs
browsing the antique shops.
I find it all so boring, but am stuck here,
a ghost in a haunted house.

At a movie about a war criminal whose American
lawyer daughter blindly defends him—blasted by the critics
because it is serious and has a message—
the audience is full of old Villagers, drawn to see it
because it's serious and has a message,
the women, no longer in dirndls and sandals,
but with something telltale about the handcrafted jewelry,
the men not in berets, but the kind that would wear them—
couples for whom being young, meant being radical,
meant free love. Anyway,
something about them says Villager,
maybe the remnants of intellect, idealism—
which has begun to look odd on American faces.

Nowadays, there's nothing radical left, certainly not
in the Village, no Left Bank to flee to, no justification
for artistic poverty, nothing for the young to believe in,
except their careers, and the fun of flaunting
their youth and freaky hairstyles in trendy enclaves.

Leftovers from the old Village, we spot each other
drifting through the ghostly
high rental picturesque streets, ears echoing
with typewriters clacking and scales and arpeggios
heard no more, and meet fugitive in coffee shops,
partly out of friendship, but also, as we get shabbier and rarer,
from a sense of continuity—like, hey, we're historic!—
and an appreciation, even if we never quite got there,
of what our generation set out to do.

MUSIC LESSONS

Tip-top on a bare tree
overlooking the wintry
supermarket parking lot
a solitary bird
pouring its heart out
breast quivering

Curious about the English word
For plain speaking wonderful
yet almost takes a miracle
born of adversity
or the kind of genius that I'm not
to make it sing

How my music teacher
with his sobbing violin
tore his hair out at my every squawk
and over my stupid head
broke bow after hopeless bow
begging me to make my cello talk

THE KUNTZES

Sometimes one of the bigger girls in the sandpit
would protect me from the tough kids,
but never Doris Kuntz — she'd beat me up herself
just for being a sissy
which insulted her idea of man.
She didn't take shit from anybody.

She was even tougher than her brother Billy
who practiced goosestepping in the back fields
where the German-American Bund held patriotic rallies
around a flagpole set in cement,
featuring swastikas, uniforms, and beer.
Crying "Viva La Bunza," he'd throw
frogs into our campfires,
and liked to remind the others I was a Jewboy
as, grinning, he socked me casually in the belly
and sent me home crying — it was that easy.

The Kuntzes were the kind that beat you up
if they knew you couldn't fight back.
It would be an easy win
to add to their scores in life —
Billy already had a sash full of merit badges
for everything from building fires by rubbing sticks
to signalling from hilltops with flags.

Of the two, Doris was the survivor.
You'd think he'd be a killer, but Billy
got shot down in the South Pacific,
and Sonny Hugg, his friend, though of a different breed —
for Sonny, other people, and frogs, had a right to live —
sentimental Sonny obtained special permission
to search for Billy's plane in the jungle.

Even back in the Depression,
when my sister went out looking day after day,
Doris was able to get a job as a secretary.
That kind of nerve was what you needed,
my mother said, with heavy irony.
Her children who lacked it understood:
there were two kinds of people
and we were the other, like our parents,
helpless before the Kuntzes of the world.

With hindsight, though, Doris could as easily
have gotten a job making lampshades
at Acme Extermination, Herr Hitler, Proprietor.

BASKETBALL LEGS

When Coach Covert said I had good
basketball legs, my heart leaped
as if I had sunk a pivot shot,
where you dribble right up under the basket
and turn and leap at the same time
to tip the ball over the rim—
which I couldn't for the life of me do.

I was the skinny jerk of the class.
When teams were being chosen
and only another boy and I were left—
him with cross eyes and a polio brace—
the captains tossed a coin.
It made no difference which of us they got.

Set shots I had to miss
because the teams lined up on either side
were watching.
Dribbling I wasn't much good at either.
The guys with longer arms
could always dance around me
and bounce the ball away with a sneer.
And if I was standing under the net
and someone yelled Field and threw me the ball,
I couldn't help it, it just bounced off my chest.

After Coach Covert's famous comment on my legs,
of course basketball became my favorite sport,
though it didn't reverse my ineptitude on the court.

SELF PORTRAIT IN THE BATHROOM MIRROR

Mystery man,
with enigmatic eyes,
who are you and what do you want?

I learn no more by putting on my glasses—
if it takes away the illusion of good looks,
it only magnifies the ravages.
Is this what the world sees?

Curious symptom of aging,
the red nose.

Hard to recognize myself.
With this face, I could be
in one of those drab, prewar British movies
where the husband, a clerk, comes home from work
to find his wife having an affair
with another dreary bloke—I could play him too—
and after the sordid confrontation on the linoleum,
sits at the kitchen table,
head in hands under the lightbulb.

Staring into my eyes,
I glimpse a robed nomad halted on a desert ridge,
his tribal face surveying like a hawk
the treeless horizon,
days from any waterhole.

Or in a cheap gray suit and tieless shirt,
I've just been released after serving time,
for molesting children, or embezzling perhaps,
and with all my possessions

wrapped in a paper bag under my arm,
walk skid row.

Or I could be an Irish workingman,
unemployed since the mill shut down,
looking straight at the camera
under the brim of my cloth cap,
grim-jawed and illusionless.

One thing is clear:
I've seen hell and it shows.

MEMORY GAP

On a theme by Taha Muhammad Ali

If I could find the dream book of the past,
of the nomadic times before Egypt, and after,
would I find a forecast of my present life?

My recurring dream of men breaking in the door,
is it just a dream?
Wasn't there a time before the desert
when I was robed and garlanded for the sacrifice
to bring on the uncertain rain?
Am I still fleeing assassins in the night
as I did before?

If my nightmares are really memories
and I could decipher them
from the ur-language of the lost book,
would they make sense of my life
with its depression, neurosis, self-hate,
in this land I find myself by chance,
or birth, or history, stranded in?

Even this language I speak
has me in knots I'm always trying to loosen —
to release my stiff jaw, unlock my joints,
set myself free from the vise
this lifetime has me in.
But then, terrifying images come in the night
that I suspect might make sense
in the mysterious tongue of the past
I do not know:
Better not try to escape this life, brother,
even if you don't belong to it,
or you're apt to go out of your mind.

What does all this mean?
And what has happened to my memory,
so that only in nightmares
do I seem real—

or is this really me?

TIRED

Never to really wake up,
this is some people's burden
that those of the tireless sort
are unable to understand, when all we want
is to lie around in a state of collapse.

First and last, I told my mother
who also suffered from it,
never use the word "tired."
It's like "depressed," a dead end—
just saying it brings it on worse.

It's as if some people don't have
an outer crust of energy
that rides over the lake of exhaustion,
a level of weariness
that is always there, threatening
to rise up and swamp us,
or that we are always in danger
of sinking into.

All our kind wants to do
is lie down and rest and sleep, bone tired,
dog tired, but never like a dog,
the lively breed that wears out people like us,
jumping up as they do, alert and ready to go,
tails wagging.

THE NOSE, OR THE WIT AND WISDOM OF JUNIOR MURPHY

We weren't ever allowed to go
to a Jimmy Durante picture show
because of all his jokes about his "schnozz."
It was no laughing matter—
terrible things were done to us because
of the shape and size,
though exactly why that was
remained mysterious. . . .
Here's a riddle: What's smack in the middle?
It's something you can't disguise
without a hammer blow and chisel,
and rhymes with Ole Man Mose?

Junior Murphy put it this way:
We were all right, he guessed,
but why did we have to breed so fast?
There were six of us kids,
so he had a point.
Killing Christ, he swore, was a rotten shame,
and besides, if you let one move in,
in no time, all the relatives came.

But when relatives visited from the city,
it was too quiet, and they fled.
And we certainly were dirty, as everybody said—
my mother believed a good heart
was everything. Still, I'd die
when anyone came into that pigsty.

He also said we loved money.
Of course we did, we were poor,
though, my mother muttered, stingy on my father's side.
Spendthrift, my father yelled every Wednesday

when her allowance ran out and she asked him
for "just a little extra" to tide her over.
He'd rant and she'd cry,
then afterwards, he'd pay.

Why shouldn't I be treated like a dog?
Didn't my father scorn the synagogue
and raise us in an "American" neighborhood,
praising Ma's straight nose as the ultimate good,
and putting down the relatives who visited
as much as Junior Murphy did?

It made me very crazy, what he and everybody said.
For years, I shlepped around my nose,
a poor son of a poor, downtrodden race,
but one day woke up—it was more complicated than that,
but let's just say I awoke, and began to understand
that being a Jew, I was rich—
I had my father, Junior Murphy, and the world to thank:
It was like discovering
I had a million dollars in the bank.

From The Booke of Shyting

"Here I sit
brokenhearted.
Paid my nickle,
and only farted."

No half-measures:
Pull down your pants
all the way to the floor.

It's odd perhaps to start with the hands
but that's a good place to get in touch,
palms together, now, as in prayer,
in this case a prayer for a good crap.
Let fingers explore each other,
pressing in the thumb —
it doesn't always have to be in charge.

Feel yourself all over,
find places that long for recognition.
Try holding your knees —
give them a steady, comforting squeeze.

Open your mouth and breathe, stretching the jaw
wider than you ever have before —
one end can set an example for the other.
Howl if you must,
as you'd do in the heat of lust,
as you did when you were born.
(A dietary tip from Indian lore:
Eat corn.)

On to the toes, beasts
carrying the burden of things,
so desolate down there,

the furthest from where you are.
Bend over and spread them one at a time,
squeezing, tickling their tips like
"This little pig. . . ."
Starting from little to big,
play each toe
in a slow ascending arpeggio,
each note corresponding
to a similar in the bowel,
and each a level of release. . . .

Think of a dog, or better yet a cow,
raising its tail, hunching into it . . .
Feel something starting now?

Reader, if this has brought it on
finish it where it belongs
behind the barn or in the john,
and dream of an orchard of figs, so ripe
they fall and squash . . .

leading to the topic when next we meet:
To Wipe or Wash?

(If Wipe, feel free to use this sheet.)

ENCOÑADO

"What's that, Ma?"
"It's where your father hit me with an axe."
"Got you right in the cunt, didn't he, Ma."

She sat on the toilet seat, legs spread,
and I helped by pouring warm water
over her cunt, bloody

as if it had been torn — in childbirth, perhaps,
each of us ripping it open
as we battered our way out with our heads,

or by the abortionist's instruments — a dozen times, she said,
not to mention Daddy, a mean fucker, if I know him,
right through blood and gore.

It was eternally bleeding — I know,
because wasn't I always being sent to the store
for the jumbo-size box of Kotex,
for which one wiseguy on the block named me Ko-Ed?

Yet, one of the wonders of nature
is that it seems endlessly repairable —
ripped open, it heals, and heals again.

And women like cats screaming
as the barbed penis rips into them, banging away,
while the Tom pants: "Oh Jewboy, that feels good."

Is there any wonder I look at it as a disaster area?

At the breast I was a biter,
which meant, "Give, damn you,"

and my fair-haired mother cursed back
at the black little bastard tearing at her breast.

This stomachache I've had all my life,
it says: Her cunt, her bloody cunt.
Yes, that will be my all-purpose curse
for headache, backache, humiliation, and failure:
Her bloody cunt, my mother's bloody cunt.

NIGHT SONG

When I get up in the night to pee
I'm no longer myself but my father—

that's when I feel most like him,
an old man going to the bathroom,

joyless, miserable, grim.
Even my urine smells like him.

Oh, I do not want to be like him.

It's as if he's crawled under my skin,
irritating, working deeper in.

Or as if we shared one skin.
Oh, how I dislike in the night becoming him.

To write this down I turn on the light,
and waking, you ask what's wrong?

Nothing, I answer, it's all right,
and by speaking become myself again.

But I'm irrevocably awake and tossing until dawn,
thinking of every stupid thing I've ever done,

and though I have to, not getting up to pee. . . .
Oh, how I hate it, hate it, being me.

ROLE MODELS
from OVER FIFTY

1.

Studying men older than me for clues
on what's ahead and how to go through it
is a grim prospect, and money doesn't help
as any visit to Miami will confirm, that paradise
full of zombies in retirement, and a bitter one, too,
from the look on their faces.
This they save up for, the wise
who pay their insurance premiums
and, congratulating themselves, move
to where their eyes go dead long before their bodies
which at least can be kept in surgical repair.

Who can hope for any better, though,
at that now-not-so-very-far-off age?
Occasionally one glimpses an old timer
with a face not consumed by rage and the injustice of it all,
with mind intact, going on with his work,
who even stands erect and looks okay,
meaning you'd hop into bed with him.
I want to throw myself at that man's feet
and, like Willie Loman to his rich brother, cry,
"How did you do it, Joe, how did you do it?"

2.

That of which I'm most afraid
is not the inevitable hearing aid,
but ending up one of the park benchers,

all of them with pacemakers and dentures,
a replacement socket for each hip,
and an aluminum walker lest I slip.

3.

To rescue at least something . . . for example,
a man I saw on the bus in France. . . .
No scraggly gray locks of the aging hippy
desperate to hold on to youth,
nor the Dapper Dan in plaid polyester
ubiquitous in the shopping plaza,
this Frenchman, at ease in his body,
wore soft fabrics of knit and tweed,
the colors of the autumn fields his eyes reflected,
and twill pants, a miracle of French tailoring —
calm, sure, and as they say, *un homme mûr*. . . .
No, that way I'll never make it,
though for style he was a master
and deserved at least the *Prix Nobel*
for aging well.

4.

Another kind of survival, then?
On television, in a Benares hospital, an Ancient One —
I don't know why I loved him but I did.

Deaf and blind maybe, wrapped in a cotton sheet,
put for the day in a chair,
already in his shroud, grateful
just to be sitting there.

Anger, grief, desire, he had let everything go,
you could see that, and his death
would be an easy slipping away,
any day now.

Clearly, this was a being of another kind,
luminous in his years,
and seeing him on the TV screen,
unexpectedly, love filled me, and overflowed in tears.

THE "OH, BROTHER" CANTATA

1.

Missing the Boat

There I stood on the shore
with my old suitcase tied with a rope,
as the hawsers fell into the water and were cranked in.

Happy passengers at the rail were waving
across the widening gap of water,
and the ship sailed off to the horizon,

growing smaller and smaller,
smoke from its funnel scrawling
TOUGH SHIT across the sky.

2.

New York Rats

Crossing Canal Street,
we dodge the trucks
like rats in the subways,
scuttling from the tracks
into drain holes
every time a train
roars through.

3.

On First Looking into the Mirror in the Morning

Not a pretty sight.

4.

The Psychology of Couples (1)

I'm so used to fighting with you
I don't know how not to.

5.

Being old is not so bad:
It all depends on having the right attitude,
for instance on catching sight of yourself in a mirror,
make a funny face,
like the fat girl who made herself the clown of the classroom
and everybody loved her.

6.

The Fault of the Jews

Gurdjieff said it takes three Jews
to make one Armenian.
Perhaps he noticed the fault of the Jews,
one that overrides half the virtues—
how we love to attract attention,
when wisdom dictates being unobtrusive.
By Gurdjieff, being a crook is okay,
the world will probably love you for it,
but for chrissake stop grabbing the microphone
and turning everything into an audition.

7.

The Psychology of Couples (2)

When sex dies
there is always one for whom desire continues—
that's always me, of course, not you.

8.

I cringe
at what Israel is doing
to the Palestinians,
and would do almost anything
to stop it,

but at least this time,
—I confess with a small, secret relief—
this time it's not being done to us.

9.

The Psychology of Couples (3)

After years together, they thought
an arrangement of a looser kind
might suit them better, so they split,
but in an unexpected twist of plot
one of them went blind
and they moved back in together again.
It could hardly be taken as a gift
yet, oddly, they were as happy then
as any two friends who ever lived—
though sex was not the key to it.

10.

The Fall of Communism

Once it was easy to brush panhandlers aside—
bums cadging drinks, left-over alcoholics from the Depression
that visiting Russians went to the Bowery to see
to prove capitalism had failed.
Further back, even, in the Depression,

I remember whole families, dispossessed,
sitting on their furniture on the sidewalks
with nowhere to go.

Nowadays, after communism has failed,
they are everywhere on the streets again,
men, women, children, and their dogs,
and who can fail to empty
pockets of change into their paper cups,
when we, too, may shortly join them?

11.

The Psychology of Couples (4)

By law,
every couple
should receive
a revolver
with two
bullets.

12.

for Sylvia

We're so lucky to have them,
these difficult darlings.

They sweep through our lives,
taking us over utterly,

making impossible demands
that we can't help
knocking ourselves out over,

still, counting ourselves lucky.

13.

"What'll It Be, Pops?"

Now that you're no longer a sex object
and probably no one will ever
have a hard-on for you again,
no longer, as you did for most of your life,
living in hopes of the future,
for there's no future anymore
that anyone could want
just as you are no longer anyone
anyone could want,
ready for the junk heap—

don't you wonder
if there isn't somewhere, anywhere,
a man of your age
is not considered garbage?

14.

The young are not as Jewish as the old.
It takes years to become Jewish,
and I mean Experience,
expressed with a loud *Oy vay,*
that in American roughly translates as
OH, BROTHER!

THE NAKED FOOL, OR, THE HISTORY OF A MOUSTACHE

Another of those electric dreams
of coming downstairs into a party
where everyone is clinking martini glasses
and chatting in well-dressed groups —
to discover that I alone
am naked like a fool.

Nobody seemed to notice, even,
or mind, but just the same,
I have since decided that at least awake
there is something I can do about it —
grow a moustache.
Why not clothe my face
that like my lower parts
also reveals my foolishness to the world?
No law says I have to be the only one around
showing everything.

What a pleasure now
to see a dashing guardsman in the mirror,
his eye so steady and true.
A hairy upper lip was all it took
to make my features more regular,
skin bronzer, teeth whiter,
and let's face it, I say, cocking my head,
it gives me the devil of a smile.

And lately, even the dream has changed.
I join the party, as usual,
a crowded ballroom, or around a pool —
but this time, reflecting the new
moustache on my upper lip, on top
I'm dressed in a shirt and tie,
but, still, below, the bareassed fool.

WORLD TRAVELLER

On the shore of the Caspian Sea
I sobbed to be so far away,
and across the plains of Turkestan,
passing camel caravans, I wept,
and in the high Pamirs, and among the ruins
of Balkh, Mother of Cities.

Desolation filled me as I saw
everywhere the men
out walking, holding hands
or with arms around each other,
friends kissing on streetcorners.

Why wasn't I happy?
I had to come to where men
were as I was, or rather where what I was
was one of the possibilities of a man.

This was the world of my ancestors
—I knew it in my bones—
ancestors whose language was lost,
and my bones were announcing
that I had suffered for nothing,
been punished for nothing.

Not only my parents had been crazy
but where I grew up was crazy—
no one could tell me different now,
I thought, as I picked up a blue tile
from the ruins and tucked it in my pocket,
rich with new-found treasures.

But no matter that I knew
—and the further I went the more I knew—
I sobbed and sobbed, for what had been done
could not, in this lifetime at least,
be undone.

VOCALISE

There is no escape, I sing,
from the pain of being me.

Uh-oh, still hung up on that? you say,
taking the superior position,

and I the foolish one
for refusing to crow
that I've worked it all through,
that I'm over it, mature now.

I wake up in the night
and know I'm not.
Admit it, don't you?

Why shouldn't I till I die
admit my pain? Mourn my life?
Complain?

You have my permission
to do it too.

Forever crippled, nervous wreck,
every day I ask myself,
Will I live?
For it surely feels like I'm dying.
These might be the last days of my life,
this, the final page.

Almost with relief now
that nothing can be done,
almost cheerfully
I sing in age:

There is no escape,
from being me.

Bio

Dear Contributor,
For our "Notes on Contributors" column, please summarize
your poetry career in 27 lines or less.
— The Editors

My first book was published finally,
after about twenty-five rejections —
I was thirty-eight by then and had been around a long time.
Naturally, in the years until,
I went a little crazy, thinking it would never happen.
Why I thought a book would rescue me
I couldn't have said. I just didn't have any other goal,
and single-minded like a lemming,
didn't know what else to do with my life.
The one thing I knew: without poetry,
life wasn't worth a sandwich.

That was in the Fifties, the epoch of "analysis,"
meaning varieties of watered-down Freud.
I spent years in "group," as we called it,
a system of mutual destruction, where the "analyst"
interpreted my "problem" as hostility masquerading as love
for the father figure you were supposed to kill,
so that you could go on to marry your mother —
it seems funny now that nobody laughed.

The "analyst" was especially dubious about my poetry
as no basis for mental health and "social adjustment,"
meaning marriage and career.
Convinced by his air-tight Oedipal logic
(I've always been a sucker for theories,
Freud, Marx, Reich, Gurdjieff, Velikovsky, et al.),
I didn't catch on that "group"
was a meat grinder and I was the lamb.

But if you survive it, you come out stronger—
that's it's main benefit.
I survived it.

Always a mediocre student,
a reader, but no intellectual,
I longed only to be one of the popular kids
instead of a jerk ("Irrepressible Eddie"
was the euphemism the yearbook used).
The sensitive type, I did my best to hide it
and clamped a pipe between my teeth like men in the ads.
Merely confused by the School of Commerce at NYU
my father had enrolled me in, I dropped out,
the war being conveniently on,
to enlist in the Air Force. They made me a clerk,
but I drank malteds for weeks to gain weight
and applied to become a fighter pilot,
still determined to show them all back home
I was no sissy. Instead, the aptitude tests
sent me to navigation school—again condemned
to a desk in the nose of the plane,
but just as scary as in the cockpit, I soon learned,
with flak bouncing the plane around
while making bombing runs over German cities.

I had grown up dreaming, like the frog-prince,
of being awakened one day—
a genius, a star,
with no work involved, of course.
But when an anthology of poetry, the Untermeyer,
was handed me by God disguised as a Red Cross worker,
at once the question What To Be When I Grow Up
was solved: Poet,
something nobody in their right minds
would ever set out to be,
so maybe it was right for me.

Stationed at an airbase in England,
I met my first real poet, Coman Leavenworth,

who was in the same class at Columbia as Allen Ginsberg,
and beat him out for The Poet Most Likely To Succeed—
it was unthinkable at that time in the literary world
where Anglo-snobbery was the rule
that anyone with the name of Ginsberg
would make it in poetry, especially at Columbia
with its quota system that had already excluded me.

I wrote T. S. Eliot a few years later
and from his mandarin eminence came the answer,
"I'm no more anti-Semitic than anti-Eskimo,"
meaning, probably, that he considered Jews
as remote from him as Eskimos—
and this was after Auschwitz,
when he wasn't in the least embarrassed
to leave anti-semitic passages in his books.

Coman was going into London on weekend passes
where he met poets at a literary club, the Gargoyle,
and though I didn't exactly put away my Rupert Brooke,
I started to read the living poets he mentioned:
T. S. Eliot, George Barker, Dylan Thomas, Harry Brown,
and Dunstan Thompson, whom I joined, starstruck, for a drink
at an east side cocktail lounge—
St. Dunstan, he could have been, with his huge eyes
and attenuated hands of an El Greco,
the aesthete I could never be, even glamorous as I was
in my Eisenhower jacket, silver wings, and battle stars.
I had to change my image.
How I admired those lines and stanzas, the wit,
the elegant tone—it wasn't all hard work, though,
it was class. I belonged to something else.

It was another poet who was to teach me how to write:
Several years later I dropped out of college again,
and on the boat to France met Robert Friend.
Sitting in cafes in Paris and Provence, we read together
from the Oscar Williams anthology, puzzling out
the curious ambiguities of modern poetry,

the mysterious ellipses, the dense language.
He looked at my poetry
and advised me to give it up.

I didn't, but somehow, it was seeing
how he worked on his own poems
that showed me how to do it for myself.
A brilliant teacher, Friend launched me, and I flew.
And found my voice.
In the tight little poetry world of those days
I began to have poems accepted by literary magazines,
William Carlos Williams gave his seal of approval
and almost immediately a book contract followed —
such luck was ominous:
it stopped my writing cold,
and the dark years of doubt began, and therapy,
when my only dream was to get back to Paris
in those post-war, bargain years,
where I could feel like a poet again —
but instead spent all my money on the analyst.
As my group kept accusing me
of wanting to run away from my problems,
I had the dream that should have let me know
which of us was crazy:
I was swimming across the Atlantic to Europe
with a pack of sharks snapping at my heels.

In the rosy illusion of psychological breakthroughs
and, not far off, promises of a wounded psyche healed,
my poetry instincts wavered,
and nothing I wrote was quite satisfying.
A strange occurrence, though, gave me hope:
One day, my father offered me money
in a way he never had before, and it was as if
a fist, long clenched, opened inside me.
I could breathe again, and a rage
of poetry poured out of me,
beginning, appropriately, with a poem called
"It is Dawn and the Cock is Crowing."

Where I had been humiliated and crushed,
something stood up proudly in me,
expressed in the final line:
"Stand up, Friend, with me."
But then the fist closed again, a weight descended,
and the brief illumination was over, never to return.
Also ended were my manic cycles,
those wonderful highs I lived for.
From then on I was forced to live in a drab, ordinary world.

Those were the years of blacklists,
travel restrictions, jailings, and even executions,
and with little hope of getting a book published,
I decided to brighten up my life by dipping
into the grabbag of old fantasies,
and trying something new.
During one of those hopeless parental discussions
about what to be when I grew up,
my mother had asked me if I wanted
to go to dramatic school, and I had to answer No,
because to admit it would
imply I thought well of myself,
and who did I think I was, wanting to be an actor?
So I became an actor, found a Method teacher,
and for several years, my life was filled
with classes, auditions, rehearsals, and performances.

My horoscope says, Trouble with publishers, and true,
it has never been easy for me to get published.
Though I had appeared in a number of magazines,
my book was rejected by one publisher after another.
I suffered, but the manuscript
was better for it—it had time to grow.
It was May Swenson, my good angel, who advised me
to make multiple submissions,
never done in the old genteel days.
But she was right. In no time,
I won the Lamont Award

and Grove Press published my first book,
Stand, Up, Friend, With Me.

Ultimately it changed my life,
but when the book, the Lamont, and a Guggenheim
all happened at once, I kept repeating:
I will not be consoled.
And of course the unloved child inside
is inconsolable, for the good reason
that you don't love the little bastard yourself.

If it was hard for me to accept success,
at least the world treated me better.
And I no longer was the family bum.
Before long, I was touring the country
giving poetry readings, arousing wonder in students
that I earned my living as a poet.
When my new therapist suggested
I bring copies of my books to sell,
I, as much of a snob about poetry as anyone,
indignantly said I was a poet, not a salesman —
but then brought books, after all:
I put them on a chair with a sign,
"Leave money and take book,"
and like magic, by the end of the reading
a pile of bills had taken the place of books.
It became my favorite part of a reading —
if they buy, it proves they love you,
and besides, a book is something you leave behind.

I had no interest in academic life,
but other projects came along: I was asked to translate
Eskimo poems for a teaching program,
because I was the only poet they could find, they said,
whose poetry was understandable by ten-year-olds.
Of course, they censored a few good old Eskimo words
like "shit" and "pee," following a law
that children must never see
words about real life in print.

My own law says that every poem should have
one unprintable word or idea in it.

I was trying everything: I wrote
narrations for a couple of documentaries,
one of which, *To Be Alive,* won an Oscar.
But films are a group effort and I'm allergic to that.
I even taught a few poetry workshops
but never felt comfortable
at either end of a classroom.
Writing reviews also seemed wrong—
I gave it up, ashamed of myself
after tearing to shreds
a few perfectly innocuous books.

Fate brought me to fiction
when my friend, a novelist, lost his sight.
I am the nurse type, anyway,
and started helping him write his books,
fulfilling a prediction by a psychic,
some years before he went blind,
that we would do something together
that would be successful.

But then people started saying
I had given up poetry to write junk.
Writing a novel does take a lot of time,
and besides, I like to take vacations from poetry,
or poetry takes vacations from me.
Writing fiction, though, was almost harder than poetry,
or collaboration was, as every word
became a war to the death—
we were ready to kill each other a thousand times,
miraculously forgotten when a chapter was done.
The rule about collaborating with someone is
it can only succeed
if nothing will break you up.
Unfortunately, the psychic did not predict

that we would end up box office poison
when a novel failed.

The trouble with writing prose
is there's so much of it.
Poetry is generally shorter,
and more manageable —
breaking up the lines of verse
keeps in order the inner thinking,
clarifies the logic.
Still, with a little electronic help
I have started writing essays,
for the word processor has the very
qualities of organization I lack,
and assembles the fragments of my scattershot mind.

Sophie Tucker used to say
I've been poor and I've been rich,
and believe me, dollinck, rich is better.
Paul Bowles too, enjoying celebrity in his old age
when most people are bitter and alone, showed me
on a visit to Tangier that, if you live,
famous in old age is better.
Odd that it never occurred to me
to want to be rich or famous.
Being a poet was enough,
though I've never believed in being too pure,
and there's no telling what I'll do next.
But the most important thing is
to go on writing poetry to the end.

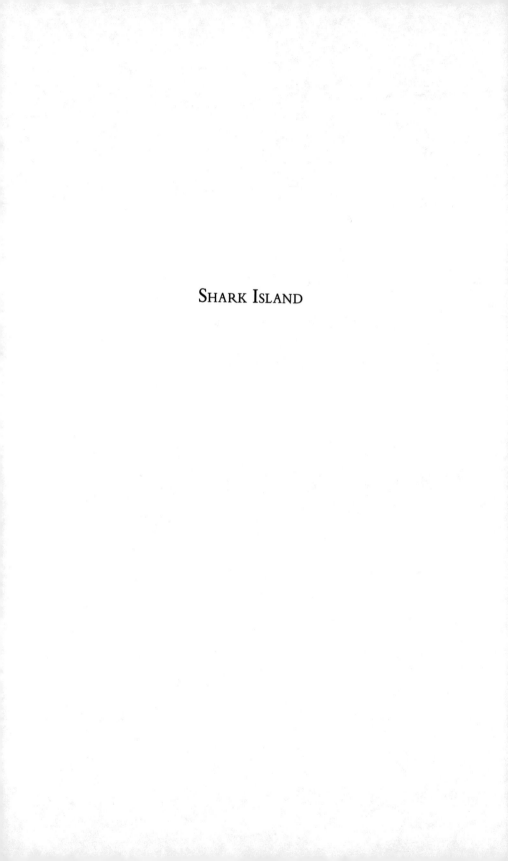

SHARK ISLAND

OH, THE GINGKOS

In this city where's it's perfectly ordinary
to pass by people collapsed on the sidewalks,
or living under plastic on park benches like gypsy camps,
or on flattened cardboard cartons in doorways,
and the gorgeous shirtless Puerto Ricans
are muttering if not raving as they brandish knives,
and high-speed bicycles, free to ignore traffic rules,
whizz by in all directions,
what, I ask you, is there to be grateful for

except the trees along the streets? And for them
we have to thank John V. Lindsay,
who was universally belittled as mayor.
Attention, Historians, when you write the books: it was he
and he alone who got those trees planted,
the only thing the eyes can bear to look at these days
in a city stinking in the summer heat
like a garbage dump.

It is hard to imagine these streets back then
without their trees. But the way I remember it,
after Lindsay was elected, the city was paralyzed by strikes—
teachers, subway and buses, garbagemen, all out,
until he was forced to play along
and made the banks happy by borrowing.
What the hell, he must have said,
what's a hundred thousand more for trees?

Oh, the gingkos he planted,
forests worth of gingkos, which only stink later
in the crisp days of fall.
Oh, the locusts, the sycamores,
oh, the stand of oak surviving the fumes in Jackson Square,

oh, the green shade of the linden trees
of Abingdon Square, now alas,
taken over by a colony of the homeless,
but that's not Lindsay's fault.

I want to say it again and again —
in a country where the government
lets its people rot on the streets,
it was Mayor Lindsay who planted the trees — and oh yes,
put this also on his tombstone, may he live a thousand years:
he stopped the police from raiding gay bars.

ENGLAND AGAIN

It's the furtiveness around the edges
that makes it exciting.
There's no question of a cosmic orgasm,
but on the other hand you aren't required
to think of it as any more
than a bit of fun
that everybody has a right to.
Dirty thoughts float around in the air
and any man, no matter how conservatively dressed,
might slip into a rubber goods shop,
fingering undergarments, flipping through magazines,
or stop to unzip and take a leak
at the massive Victorian marble public urinals
where rows of wankers greet the eye,

before rushing off to address parliament
or be presented to the Queen.

RULE OF THE DESERT

1.

All night on the bus, crowded three to a seat—
the government bus, a bargain—
the metal edge of the window rubbed my elbow raw.
Over and over, through the dry heat of the desert night,
I said the 23rd Psalm . . . green pastures . . . still waters.

Hours of this, until a midnight rest stop
for tea under trees strung with dim lights
by a dark hotel, alone on the vast, barren plain.
A Russian resort, the waiter said,
but they came only in winter.
And over there? I asked, pointing to a wall.
The swimming pool, he said.
Full? I asked.
Of course, he said.

A pool? But I had no bathing suit, no towel,
and we'd be leaving in a few minutes,
the night-long drive ahead. I sat,
thirst unquenched by the tea, the last orange
from Herat. Debated. Yes . . . No . . . Impossible.
Then walked over to the wall
where a line of turbanned men from the bus
were waiting for departure, and sure enough,
there was a swimming pool, deserted, dark.
At once, I was over the wall, sweaty clothes off,
and slipped into the water—pure water from springs
far beneath the desert, silvery in moonlight.
Not a turbanned head turned round.

On the bus again, instantly dry in the desert air,
I pondered the miracle of it—after hours of prayer,
a Russian swimming pool in the desert?
Still, this was the East, where mysterious
things can happen—one minute beggar, king the next.
And perhaps here, if you pray correctly—if, if,
allowing for many ifs and not expecting anything,
certain prayers might be answered.

2.

After that, no one would talk to me
except a French girl, going to stay with nuns,
who asked to sit next to me for protection.

By the others, I was made to feel
I had disgraced myself with violations
of dignity, modesty, manliness.

There are rules in the civilized world,
and even if I was a tourist
(the driver muttered the word), wasn't I a man?

Clearly, the French girl was also disgraced,
sitting as she was with me in the men's section—
the worse offender, even,
and by association, a whore.

But by the time the bus broke down at dawn
and before we were picked up by another,
I was forgiven. The men nudged me, grinning,
saying, "How many times?"
indicating the frightened girl,
now properly up front with the veiled women,
as I was in back with the heavy-breathing men.

For Tobias Schneebaum

Letters from an adventurous friend describe
his visits to a naked stone-age tribe
(all smeared with pig fat and for my tastes skinny)
surviving in the forests of New Guinea.
My friend explores what usually is missed
by the explorer or the scientist.

Enough, then, about carved shields and deadly spears,
spiral inserts for the nose and ears,
which make the tribesmen unglamorously fierce,
foot-long penis sheathes they wear erect
that anthropologists eagerly collect —
things with which I've always been slightly bored
and the secrets I want to hear about ignored.

Now my friend confirms what one suspects:
there's more to primitive life than artifacts,
or head hunting, or eating human brains —
though he assures me a lot of that remains.
An appealing custom my friend has learned about
from his stone-age friends — first hand, no doubt,
though the missionaries claim they've wiped this out:
of the ancient traditions that endure,
one holds that a boy can't properly mature
unless he ingests an unspecified amount,
but the more the better, of jungle gism
spurting fresh and joyful from the fount —
good for a growing boy's metabolism.
What's more, the future of the tribes depended
on keeping their boys kneeling or up-ended.
So the men of this people wisely do their best,
my friend writes, in the tribal interest

to help each growing boy become a man,
shooting a load as often as they can.

Pig fat and all, the primitive world of sex,
for those, like my friend, with the nerve to risk their necks.

POST MASTURBATUM

Afterwards, the penis
is like a girl who has been "had"
and is ashamed.

Sudden neglect, you goose,
after all those romantic promises,
carried off by soft caresses,
before the hard ramming
when you bit your lip until it was over—
foolish one who gave in,
went all the way . . .

until the next time,
when the nudge of a lover's ardor,
or the sight of it,
and the memory of something
genuine if painful
are again convincing.

TEMPTATION

He dreamed that a policeman
stood over him with a club
to make sure he didn't get a hard on.
Getting control over it
had been his life's goal
back in those schooldays
when the greatest humiliation
was being called to the blackboard
with his pants sticking out
and the boys snickering,
or getting one in the crowded showers,
where to follow the impulse in the hand
would be suicidal—
as in the dream if he
reached out and groped the cop.

She lit another cigarette
from the burned-down stub:
What a droll idea
to look for love in a toilet,
don't you agree? she said
as we sat in a London pub.

I didn't, and instead
of keeping quiet
should have replied:
But that's where love first lifted
its legendary head—
like cyclops, one-eyed,
and like a Templar helmeted
and welcomed me into the club.

The Veteran

Even before the fear of blackmail and police,
being beaten up, strapped in for shock, and worse,
the humiliation of being dragged whimpering into the open,

the boyscout manual promised
that it would drive you crazy,
which didn't keep me from uncontrollable
beating off under the covers.

The army kept showing a film of chancre sores,
raw meat penises, rotten tongues held out with forceps,
a guy who could only whisper hoarsely
for us not to make the mistake he did—
and a million times I was convinced
I caught something in every sneaky sex act.
Oh, the heart-sinking disgust
of coming up with a crab-louse in the tweezers,
pale legs in slow motion.

How could it not have come, then, to this,
the ultimate punishment of AIDS, an inner voice argues—
even while good sense says it's just a disease,
not a moral judgment.

Caught in crystal like a prehistoric insect
that lived but never quite flew,
the mineral hardening around him,
it's with regret, but truthfully also relief,
that this old veteran—masturbator, midnight stalker—
fed up with it from a lifetime of guilt and worry,
can at last take his discharge,
and put sex away, probably forever.

To the Sun

Already on the plane they seem stupider,
fight over seats, demand service,
as if in a country where every moment
you must plot your advantage—
though it does feel like we are being processed.

Perhaps, troublemakers, they are refusing that,
refusing not to be human, refusing to be simplified.
Like the cab driver from the Soviet Union—
when I told him what route to take,
refusenik, he refused. Russia was lucky
to be rid of him, but for that, we have to suffer?

Landing, I find that the coconut palms have all died,
and everyone only seemed concerned
with shopping and surgery. If these Jews
are low level, one feels America made them so.
Supposed to be smart, what happened?
Once they read Tolstoy, had dreams,
went out on picket lines. . . .
Difficult, okay, there's no law
against a Jew being a pain in the ass,
or different, or oblivious to social graces . . .
but where did the curiosity go, the mental restlessness?
Could an Einstein come out of this place, I wonder,
as I hand over my credit card at the counter?
In these airconditioned malls, how one longs
for the ozone of ideas, or just the BBC World Service,
static and all . . . Damn, I left the little
shortwave radio home, my lifeline to . . . to elsewhere.

Here in the relentless sun there is no elsewhere—
this is it. To survive,

I clutch the return ticket, repeat the date in my mind,
praying that the city where my life is, such as it is,
is still there, that escape is possible—

and that this is not the inevitable future.

SHARK ISLAND

Biff Harmon, specialist in shark behaviour,
had a tank full of them at the ocean lab,
killers he swam among and fed by hand.

Wilma was pure California
with her sun-kissed plumpnesses, coming in
as Biff was drying himself off
for a quick fuck beside the tank, as the sharks
went wild, bellies up, gnashing their teeth on the glass.

Biff planned an expedition to a Central American lake
with a fresh-water shark never before studied.
To pacify the shark spirits
the natives still made sacrifices,
human in the old days, and after the priests came,
animals fed on hot peppers—the sharks seemed satisfied.
But this year, the corn and beans have not grown.
The pigs have all been fed to the sharks, even the scruffy
village dogs, and the villagers are desperately
casting eyes around for a power offering . . .

Wilma walked through the marketplace in minuscule shorts
that outlined the cleft of her pussy and ass, tempting the Gods.
Old women in shawls and bowler hats sat impassive
in front of their peyote buttons and magic mushrooms,
and the men did not acknowledge her presence,
but all understood, as dark eyes met
(it floated into their heads at the same time),
that soon the crops would grow again.

Biff started his research cautiously
with a steel cage lowered into the lake's shark grounds.
They snapped the rods like cornflakes—the pepper-fed dogs

had only whetted their appetites.
Not enough for them the occasional washerwoman
or the scrawny child wading they could sneak up on.
And when Wilma and Biff went out in a boat to see the sunset,
beneath them the message "white meat" flashed
from shark to shark like heroin over their radar.

The lovers were unable to resist each other,
alone in the flimsy rowboat in the setting sun
that gave a rosy tint to the full breasts exposed to Biff.
Wilma spread her legs over the sides and fell back under him,
but when they climaxed in the rocking boat
her love cry turned into a scream, as teeth
chomped on her ankle, and his yelp of joy into a shriek,
as her cunt clamped on him.
Without much room for mobility, Biff
hit out at the shark as best he could with an oar.

Luckily it was a young one, not Tumba, king of the sharks,
and Wilma wasn't badly hurt,
but her blood was in the water, mixed
with the blood-red setting sun reflected there.
That taste was super-crack to sharks
and every one of them, especially Tumba, had a bead on her.
Wherever she went, even on land,
they tracked her from the lake with their radar.

On a moonless night the festival was declared,
chosen by the shaman to coincide with Wilma's period.
The villagers floated the raft-shrine on the lake's black waters
as drums made the air reverberate in torchlight
and fins circled in intricate patterns.
A thud, and Biff was out cold, tied up
on the dirt floor of a hut. Wilma, doped
with a cocktail of psilocybin, ayahuasca, and snakeroot,
was decked out in the ancient sacrificial costume,
her genitals exposed. On the raft, the shaman
pulled out her tampax so the menstrual blood would flow,

inviting the great shark, Tumba,
to nose in and feast, and bring luck to all.

Just as the noble Montezuma was betrayed
by one of his own and his empire destroyed,
Biff's faithful assistant Mungo, son of the shaman,
untied his hands and together they sneaked to the jungly shore,
parting the shrubbery to peer through: out on the raft
the shaman was doing something odd with his dick,
but nothing cruel, just part of an ancient rite,
waving it around at Wilma to consecrate her cunt.
He had an impressive tool, though he was a runt,
and Wilma giggled away, high as a kite.

If only the boys could swim out there under water,
they'd have a chance of grabbing her away—but the sharks. . . .
Here Mungo became invaluable with his native lore.
He had a vial of extract of the rare shark orchid,
that, spilled into the water, would repel the sharks awhile.
It was a trick his father used
to make people think he had power over sharks.
Slipping the vial into his loin cloth, Mungo, followed by Biff,
swam underwater to the raft, crowded with villagers
and surrounded by sharks, gathered for the sacrifice,
where Mungo opened his vial and repelled the sharks,
giving the two men time to get hold of the raft
and tip it over.

Towing the giggling Wilma by the hair,
they swam like mad to the far shore,
while the sharks for once were busy gorging
on all the human meat they wanted, the floundering villagers.
Glancing back, Biff saw the bedraggled feathered headdress
follow the shaman's feet into the hungry maw
of the ancient killer, Tumba, who then lunged
after the stoned white bride promised as the sacrifice.

It was faithful Mungo who fought Tumba in shallow water,
barely able, before he was devoured, to wave farewell

130

as Biff and Wilma clambered up the bank,
hacked their way through miles of jungle to the road,
and hitchhiked back to civilization.

DIRTY OLD MAN: TWO VARIATIONS

1.

When I go senile, I swear I'm going to let go
and grope everything in sight—
the Italian waiter in his black trousers,
that soulful-eyed hasid at the discount store,
the doctor leaning close to take my blood—
what I've had to hold back on all my life.

So what if they put me away
in a nursing home?
I'll feel up the attendants,
who may well think,
Why not let him? Don't do me no harm.

2.

For once in my life
I'm going to be free
and grope everything in sight:
let them cut off my hands, palms
still hairy from adolescent onanistic bouts,
I'll grope with my toes—
they'll have to amputate them one by one.
Then my tongue, my lips, my toothless gums.

Let them take away part after part,
something forbidden is still possible
with kneecaps, elbows, ears—
every part of me has a dirty mind.
And through it all I'll stare my fill
right up to when they seal my eyes.

They can cut out my heart, of course,
but even that's no guarantee:
my newly-liberated senile ghost
will go a-roving day and night.
And then what's to stop me groping
every man in sight?

ROCKABILLY

I wanna be your jockey shorts
that hold your cock and balls,
I wanna be your underwear
and be there when it falls,
releasing all the bounty of
your bouncy genitals.

I want to cup your downy cheeks,
squeeze between, and sniff and taste,
and run my elastic band like greedy
fingers round your waist . . .
I wanna be your jockey shorts
that hold your cock and balls,
I wanna be your underwear
and be there when it falls,
and watch you shaking out
your soft and bouncy genitals.

And when you slip your hand in,
I'll caress you fore and aft,
feeling your foreskin sliding
up and down the shaft . . .
I wanna be your jockey shorts
that hold your cock and balls,
I wanna be your underwear
and be there when it falls
in a heap to the ground in worship of
your bouncy genitals.

And when it rises throbbing
aganst my cotton knit,
I'll stretch and let it fill me up
and when it shoots drink all of it . . .

I wanna be your jockey shorts
that hold your cock and balls,
I wanna be your underwear
and be there when it falls
all in a sweaty heap beneath
your juicy genitals.

It cheers me up to see a pair of buns,
and breaks no law, spotting the better ones.

◄ • ►

If I go blind, he said,
I'm getting me
a roving-eye dog.

◄ • ►

Song of the Toke

Give me a puff of your cigarette
and I'll look in your eyes until dawn.

◄ • ►

A boy in his fresh youth
    is a pretty thing, he said,
        and for some a hot number,

but I prefer a man,
    not just in his years of ripeness,
        but even into the goatish vigor of old age.

◄ • ►

Wet Dream

Often in dreams I make love
with a dog or a horse.

136

In the middle of a kiss
animal mouth turns to lips

and everything works in harmony
to a perfect orgasm.

◄ • ►

Stroker

If you're a man, that's a cock in your hand,
your own, of course, but no different
from stroking anyone else's —
it's still a throbbing prick
you're giving pleasure to,
a schvantz you're having fun with.
So whatever your fantasies
of pussy, tits or panties,
jacking off in reality
is a homosexual act,
the main difference being
that the wanker,
and probably this means every man,
is queer for himself.

◄ • ►

Brief Bio

A boy who is an inveterate hitchhiker
cannot fail to learn about sex.

◄ • ►

Tell it to the Marines

When the Marine Corps convoy
was stalled for hours, he told me,
his buddy left him at the wheel

and went down the line of trucks,
giving blow jobs
to one bored driver after another.

◄ • ►

Male Manifesto

Coming is overrated, and in the long run
falls into the category of a good sneeze.

The body's best trick is erection,
holding up the universe on your finger.

Natural Desire

It's not a cosmic earthquake
and never was for me,
though I know that that's what others make
their sex lives out to be,
as if for them the angels sing
a continual hosanna:
for me, it's a small and lovely thing,
important in its arena.
But everything I've ever done
has been from natural desire.

Even so, I criticize
my love-life too easily.
Ashamed, I tend to minimize
and label it as measly.
Why couldn't the Lord have been
more generous for once
and doled me out a bigger one. . . .
Would I really have more fun
or wouldn't it make a difference?
Hasn't everything I've done
been from natural desire?

With all the propaganda
of what it's supposed to be,
I simply have to stand up
and do what's right for me.
If it's grown-up sex that others do
and what I do is not—
still, haven't I done what I wanted to,
fooled around dirty a lot?
Everything I've ever done
has been from natural desire.

SPACE OPERA (A FRAGMENT)

The Count ordered a dragon ship
to fly him into the zone of insurrection.
Black Orgel must not escape, he said.
His balls will dangle from my sceptre
or my name's not Count Honkie.
He threw his scarlet cape back, adjusting
the oxygen bubble on his head
and strode out to the launching pad.

Orgel was the leader of the black hominoids,
natives of the planet Usa
that the white spacemen, led by Count Honkie,
had conquered and were colonizing.
Now rebellion had broken out, and with Orgel in command
a group of the hominoids had fled to the Sierras,
taking with them as hostage Desira, beautiful
white spacewoman whom Count Honkie
had been chasing all over the universe,
but she kept brushing him off.
Her tight white spacesuit tantalized his dreams
especially where the parachute harness
pulled up between her legs and crossed over her breasts,
forcing them apart. How those beauties
strained at the fabric, crying for freedom. . . .

Pull yourself together, Honkie, he commanded himself.
Save Desira from the black hominoids
and in gratitude she'll come across. Anyway, after Orgel
and his hominoids get through with her
she won't be such a proud virgin. Those long legs
will be spread by more than parachute straps —
hominoids are hung like bulls, and merciless.

He called his lieutenant Dagon, a young metoso,
a halfbreed between spaceman and hominoid.
Metosos were always loyal to the whites
since their own kind rejected them.
Dagon zoomed over with his shoulder jets
and smartly saluted his boss who looked him over . . .
the cafe-au-lait complexion and perfect build
with those round buttocks and quite a fat
basket of goodies where it mattered.
These modern spacesuits had a way of clinging
that made your fingers itch, and your mouth
water with the juiciness of it all.
But hell, Dagon was a lousy metoso. His spaceman father
must have been atomized for screwing with a hominoid.

Dagon, he commanded, arm the men with chemical weapons.

Which formula, sir, oblitera or plastica?

Plastica. We want them docile, not dead. Even Orgel . . .
I want his balls dangling from my sceptre tonight,
but keep him alive. . . . Honkie laughed diabolically.

Evil Dagon saluted, the dragon ship arrived
on the elevator from the underground hangar,
and the space troops and their leader
got in and spun off.

Meanwhile in the Sierras of the rebel planet
Black Orgel and his band of hominoids
were preparing to torture their lovely captive Desira
to get the secrets of white power out of her.
They spread her out against a boulder,
staking her hands and feet. She strained
against the ropes and her nipples
stood up in fear as Orgel loomed over her
with his bush of nappy hair haloing his pointed head.
Clinging to his massive shoulders was his woman,

Nympha, her white pointy teeth bared in hatred
as she looked at the proud spacewoman defying her captors.

What you got that we don't got, Orgel demanded,
brandishing a turkey feather at her privates.
Technology, Desira replied for the hundredth time.
But technology was something hominoids couldn't grasp—
they lacked a cell in their brains for the idea of it.
The hominoids had been living an idyllic simple existence
when the spacemen, fleeing their own devastated planet,
arrived in their dragon ships,
raining down a fiery death before landing,
to intimidate any possible inhabitants.
Of all the planets in the sky, they had ascertained
that Usa was most favorable for settlement.

Just as Orgel and Nympha were about to tickle
a truth they could understand out of Desira,
the dragon ship flew overhead, the spotter apparatus
focussing on the rebel band,
and the loudspeaker blared, Surrender, hominoids,
at which they cowered on the ground, hissing and foaming,
unable to resist the spacemen's magic. . . .

The Spoiled Coast

My first impression on the bus
was Miami Beach, but Spanish,
with flocks of the Spanish old, dressed in black,
out walking, walking under winter palm trees, steady as camels.
Worse, as the bus swerved along the coast,
were the mile after mile of garish hotels and villas
obliterating the landscape, the clutter
of restaurants and tourist shops that the off-season
made more tacky for being Closed or For Rent —
it could be anywhere I ever wanted to flee from.

But at sundown, through the bus windows,
the stony mountains, that all day hung sullen in the distance,
loomed up with a dark clang against the sky,
and to the clicking heels of flamenco
from the driver's cassette deck,
tiled roofs, cypresses and fir trees
sang in the hoarse, triumphant voice
of the Andalusian night.

THE REPRIEVE

Away for a month, I knew something was missing,
but just couldn't put my finger on it.
Why should I feel confused in this foreign city,
so clean and orderly after New York, so safe,
so civilized? Instead, I'm like one of those writers
ransomed from the Nazis—one day the concentration camp,
the next Hollywood, lounging by a swimming pool
under palm trees in the sun,
where the nightmare is still the reality.

In this city of no roaches, I'm sickened by the memory
of what I'll soon be going back to, the exploding
bug population, part of daily life there,
among all the problems in the world,
surely not the greatest, I try to tell myself—where,
still vulnerable from dreams, with your morning hard-on,
to have to start swatting them
around the kitchen sink, the counter. . . .
In fear, they panic,
and you are the whips, the dogs,
the barking commands, the blinding lights,

and in the confusion, how hard they run,
for life is sweet to them.

HAPPY LANDINGS

Coming home is coming down:
the apartment is burgled, friends
have committed suicide, died of cancer,
or moved away, and those left
are depressed as they were before, but I'd
forgotten that while off coping
with the wholesome basic problems of the traveller.

The streets are filthy and the air foul,
my throat is raw and I feel generally poisoned.
The post office didn't forward the mail
but jammed it into the box, urgent business
that needed immediate attention long ago.
And the man next door has taken to playing his music loud.
I lie here cursing as it vibrates through the wall.
Is this home or is it hell?

Sleep anyway is impossible
due to jet lag and the time-zone change,
so I get up before dawn to an empty refrigerator,
go out through perilous streets in the final stages
of desperation from the night before
to a lunch counter for first breakfast,
fried and indigestible.

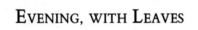

EVENING, WITH LEAVES

EVENING, WITH LEAVES

For Ack and Barbara

From Dutch rooftops, pigeons in summer rut
are burbling of lust, while a cat
crouched on the toolshed looks up with yellow eyes
through branches at the blackbird
defending its territory (if that's what birdsong means)
with a whistling that for me
wins first prize from nightingales.

In the enclosed yard every bush and tree,
loaded with leaf and flower, responds
in its individual way to the wind
that brings a fresh smell of cows from the polders,
and shakes the golden raintree blossoms
into the uncut grass with its own crop
of new seed, silver in twilight.

Aphids swarm on the dahlias,
drinking a sticky sap,
and I lurch with a groan
out of canvas sling chair
to hose them off, idly rubbing
leaf ribs and crisp tips clean,
soaking my sneakers,

then play the spray on the sagging fence
to wet down the darkening compost heap,
as the last boat gives three honks from the harbor,
leaving for England.

HOLLAND

1.

If some trickster of destiny left you a swamp
and you wanted to make a country out of it,
call in the Dutch,
for that is what they're brilliant at.
Their own country is entirely man-made,
works perfectly, looks spiffy,
and better than the Emperor's nightingale
real birds sing.

2.

Cities built on sand, yes,
but theirs stay—at least as long
as any others are apt to these days.

3.

Who would have thought
that flat could be so satisfying, you think,
as the neat little train
hisses smoothly over its tracks?

4.

When a stink invades your train compartment,
don't look at your shoes or glare at your neighbors.
It is only the fields outside
being spread with what they have lots of—

cow-, horse-, sheep-, and pigshit,
covering the sandy sea floor for tulips to grow in.

5.

Now that Little Black Sambo is outlawed,
the Dutch and the Eskimos are the two races left
suitable for children—one from where the sun
shines six months steady and six more not,
while children, adorable in fur,
shoot bows and arrows at snowmen.
The other, with even less sun, but with bright flowers
to disguise the fact, has the number one contender
for all-time children's hero, the boy
with his finger in the dike. It is easy
to ignore the wife-swapping in the igloo nights,
as we overlook the shit-littered streets here
and exclaim how neat and clean it all is.

But both love children to have a good time,
and the parents are always smiling, smiling.

6.

They are the kindest people in Europe,
perhaps because they've had to rise
above such rotten luck—not only in the matter
of the swamp, but imagine
being next door to the German army. Dear,
there's no other word for it, they're dear—
the lady on the train who saved the Jews, the youth
giving you directions with such serious eyes,
you can't resist the desire to ravish him.
And even if you meet them only for a moment,
the Dutch are so dear
you miss them forever.

THE SHINING

in memoriam May Swenson

it was something unearthly

how her head

always appeared

to shine

glowing with light

as if haloed

wild creatures sometimes

with their alert

goodnatured eyes

looking over

the rims of nests

of pinecones feathers bones

or popping up

from holes in sheared lawns

to the despair

of some

the delight

of many

have heads like that

a cap of smooth

fur that catches the

light

and just when you can

no longer resist

reaching out

                                    to pet

if not possess

with a playful

                                    whisk of a tail

and the wink

                                    of an eye

they're gone

CALLAS

The voice that came out of her
chose her as its earthly vehicle,
for reasons only the gods can know.

She spoke of it as separate from her, a wild creature
she had to struggle to master.

It floats like an unwieldy bird with a small head,
whose wings can't quite control the over-large body
soaring dangerously low above jagged peaks,
wobbling in the updrafts.

An Egyptian sculpture of a priestess,
she held up her large, arresting hands,
invoking the authority of the ancients —
hawks, serpents, bulls and suns surrounded her as she sang,
cut into stone.

She had that specialized genius for song
birds have, an intelligence of too high a vibration
for the practical matters of life.
But she was unfaithful to her gift —
even if for the perfectly understandable reasons
of being fashionable and getting a man —
otherwise she would never have dieted down,
but stayed fat for those spectacular tones,
living only for art.

It was an operatic fate
that the man she suffered over
was one of the great rats
who dismissed the most magnificent voice in the world
as just a whistle in her throat.

But after her sexless marriage, this was probably
the first man with a hard on she got together with,
and duck-like, fixated on, as is so common with us ordinary slobs.
With some men, whatever they are besides, the cock
is the best part of them, even if they are monsters
and, like him, supremely ruthless.
And perhaps his selfishness is what ravished her,
for it was sex in the raw, the one thing
singing wasn't.

Like Norma, the Druid nun, who broke her vows
for the love of a mere mortal,
she, too, was cast aside,
not for any high priestess, but a more
earthly rival, famous widow, jet set icon,
who didn't need his powerful cock, just his power,
and to get her hands on his bank account.

She threw away her magic voice for a man who threw her away,
thunderclap in the heavens, an accusing dagger of lightning,
and her crystal brain—
whose single-minded command like a bird's
was to soar, to sing—
shattered, and she fell.

NOWHERE

—after Flavia Cosma

Such a beautiful state we have founded
whose resonant name is Nothing.
Exhausted veterans of rewritten history,
stifling in our shabby houses,
we grasp at memories,
but they're so trivial, like ashes,
that we decorate them with bright rags
to try to cheer ourselves up.
Flickering in the air, these ghosts
possess us—our actions
belong to their dream.
So we live on, burdened with our lives,
without hope, without pride—
but O, this dream world,
how large, how beautiful it is,
isn't it?

Is it too late, dear friends,
to make an end of this—
burn all flags, strip off masks,
find another way to live,
where illusions blind us no more,
where deafened ears
hear again the sea's murmuring,
where the crippled
run, and oh, the wicked
weep?

THE TIME BOMB

From the very first, the moment of commitment,
it starts ticking, but fool that you are
it takes you years to realize the fact
that you have fallen into a trap,
the trap time set for people like you,
a joke accompanied by unheard cosmic laughter.

Not knowing what was in store, how you revelled
in having someone of your own at last,
in your daily life together, rejoicing
at having escaped your hated solitary existence,
that state of loneliness painfulissimo —
all the while, in your new bliss, ignoring
what was only too evident all around you, the red-
eyed, angry bereaved, living out their lives alone.

You live as if it wouldn't ever happen to you . . .
it's light years off, isn't it? And then
it dawns on you, like the snake entering the garden,
that one of you has to go first,
that as night follows day
one must die before the other —
and too much to hope for, the lucky accident
that carries you both off together.
Once perceived, a justifiable cause, I'd say, for divorce,
at least for the many unable to face a future
of counting backwards towards finality.
Why not, then, be a fancy dancer, and keep splitting up
and starting again — another lover, a new marriage,
expertly breaking off with each in time?

But for you now, there is no escape.
And how your single years, that once seemed such a waste

you devoted most of your income to expensive therapies,
desperate just to find someone, get hooked up—
"till death do us part," as you, poor fool,
swore in your silly heart, not knowing, never guessing—
yes, you poor, poor fool, how your former life
of multiple sex partners (even if in their thousands
they couldn't fill the lonely heart, or all the lonely hours)
doesn't, in the light of what's ahead,
seem such a pitiful fate, and, indeed,
though you wouldn't go back to it again for anything,
appears, if not luckier, then less anguished.

THE GUIDE

How I loved the high country, the snow, and the cold,
and with such pure air it was exhilarating,
the two of us setting off across the valley
dotted with clumps of spruce,
and even with his handicap, it was easy
to guide him through the deep, powdery snow
that the wind blew up in our faces.

Then the land rose, and with his handicap
the going got harder, but he held onto my shoulder
and we slogged on to the top
where we stopped, breathless: below
was a terrible, almost perpendicular, drop
into a landscape shattered by some ancient cataclysm,
a jumble of rocks with dangerous crevices
hidden by snow, and twisted trees
clinging everywhichway.

I stood there, aghast, and calculated:
we could camp here overnight,
but even if we managed, holding on,
to slide and tumble down the slope
without breaking anything,
and by some miracle end up together,
how, with his handicap, could I guide him
through the rocky terrain ahead—though I knew
there was no way to go, but on?

GARBO

Her eyes never blink—
higher beings do not blink,

nor people in remote lands
who stare at you from the fields—
but that's innocence, like animals.

If blinking is a kind of flinching,
she never flinches.
She doesn't adopt any facial expression—
it's her feelings she shows
or none at all. Nor does she put on
mannerisms like we do, meaning
we're desperate for attention.
If she says she wants to be alone
she's the only one we believe it of.

It's no devices then that make her beautiful
but the lack of them. Still, the awkwardness
of her grace shows that being graceful
is not an easy victory—
there's the permanent mournfulness in the mouth
and the testimony of those eyes—
no blinking it back,
it's all there.

Can't we make the same commitment,
risk shedding evasions, devices, defences
—in short, our faces—
and look unblinking at each other, vulnerable
to what in our hearts we long for,
whatever the cost, wherever it leads?

Or does she affirm that for mere mortals
the price is too great,

though for herself
she could not, would not, choose another fate.

THE FINAL VISIT

I flew down because they were worried:
there she lay, ancient as parchment,
eyes sunken into her head, in a doze.

Part of her dentures were gone
but the beauty of her facial bones remained,
as well as the dents in her skull where they drilled in —
terrible things are done to keep them alive, the old ones.
But that is all in the past. Now,
we let her alone
with a twenty-four hour nurse.

There's no longer much communication
between her state and ours.
Hand fed, she enjoys eating — at least she says "More" —
but she's not bothering with my trivial questions.
"Not interested," she says, like a ouija board
in a voice from another dimension.
Her mind only seems to work if it is engaged.
To test her, I ask what she thinks of Reagan,
and out snaps, "He's the worst."
And when I sing an old song, she smiles
and, eyes shut, sings along,
then gets rid of us by saying she has to go on the commode.

To justify her addiction to dexies, she always said,
"For thousands of years, mankind
has been striving for perfection.
He's gone a long way toward it
but is not perfect yet. Until then,
you need a pill."

She has a legal regimen of pills now,
but I don't think that is what keeps her somnolent.
It's simply that, at last, she's getting enough rest.
While raising six children,
never having to do anything was her lifelong dream.
Though she dreaded ending up like her own mother
who took to her bed years before she died.
Still, her mother was a wise woman,
and sleeping away the years
of pain and uselessness may be best.

Now she gives off an undeniable atmosphere of comfort
and in fact even murmurs, "I'm comfortable."
The message is clear: Do Not Disturb.
Watching her, I feel I am getting lessons
in how to rest, in being at rest.

She used to say, "I'm still searching for the answer,"
and I want to ask, "Have you found it, Ma?"
Is this state simplicity regained—
of her childhood in Poland,
an ocean, a continent, a lifetime away?

The phone call came a week later.
She must already have been dying when I saw her,
so I know that for her it was not a painful death.
Just before the end she even said to the nurse,
"Send in my husband," as if at last
all was settled on that score too
and she was ready to join him.

Now, alive or dead, it's okay, Ma,
I know you found peace.

THE STUMPS

We parked in the driveway, my sister and I,
and just sat there, looking
at the house where they had lived.
The FOR SALE sign was not yet up.

Her lawn chairs were still outside,
corroded, the webbing already rotting,
and the stumps of the two pine trees in front
that he cut down for fear that in a storm
they would crash down across the roof—
he was always worried about the roof
and, almost to the end, in his eighties,
climbed up to scrape mold off the tiles and paint them.

A dead branch of the flame tree
lay on the lawn, but the mango and avocado
were gloriously green again, as they hadn't been for years,
for he kept trying to poison them—
if they died the city would cut them down for free—
so the leaves always looked sparse and the bark blasted.

It was only the trees that made the house distinctive,
especially the two pines, now mere stumps in the lawn,
and the blue metal storm blinds that once were bent awry
by a hurricane outside the room where I slept
on my duty visits there—I won't say home,
for this was never my home—but in that room
I always had wet dreams like a boy.

After his kidneys failed, and her head operation,
she lived there, bedridden, with only a woman
to look after her, waiting for death.

Unseen and uncared for, his garden went scratchy
and the roof tiles darkened with mold.

Looking in the rearview mirror at the lines around my eyes,
as I back out of the driveway,
I think, with no tears, they were never happy here.
The house stands more as a memorial to that fact
than to them, as it again waits
for new occupants, another retired couple probably,
to live out whatever is left of their lives.

LETTER FROM A FRIEND

for Harry Goldgar

"I have an idea for an E. Field-type poem, although
not being a poet, I must depend upon you to write it —
if, that is, you share the sentiment.

It's about the 'collapse of communism'
which everyone has been celebrating for months.
Well, yes, of course it had to go —
but I am sorry about it.

I mean I am sorry for the failure
of the utopian ideal. I am sorry
for the ghosts of Lenin and all those folks
who were seized, possessed, by this dream
and tried to put it into practice,
make it work,

and who tried for 70-odd years, or a hundred,
if you want to go back to the beginnings,
and after all that effort, it just didn't pan out.

It's all very well to say, superciliously,
that they should have known
it was impractical and couldn't work, but still,
isn't it a pity, isn't it sad

that this enormous experiment
in making the world better
has flopped?"

Dear friend, I couldn't say it better.

166

THE SCREAM

AIDS IS GERM WARFARE AGAINST HOMOSEXUALS
screamed the poster, pasted up around the city,
probably hand-printed in a cellar by some certifiable crazy
making connections, out of a terrible clarity of mind—
like the revolving red flashes of alarm
of a police car careening through the streets—

CIA PLOT . . . KENNEDY ASSASSINATION . . .
PENTAGON . . . FUNDAMENTALISTS . . . SECRET LABS
. . . BIOLOGICAL ENGINEERING . . . EQUATORIAL
AFRICA . . . HUMAN GUINEA PIGS,
it cries,

and all it took was a few
doctored poppers sold at bathhouses
in New York and San Francisco,
and in no time, sexual freedom
and its easy pleasures,
gone,

not to mention, the poorer and darker populations,
and as a bonus, drug addicts.

It's crackpot, of course, hard to believe
anyone was loony, or criminal, enough, to manufacture
this virus, much less release it among us.
More likely, it's only nature's latest attempt
to reduce the population, in which case
it doesn't matter who gets it in the neck
or how it spreads.

But why then did they have to arrest the poster man
and put him away for saying what he believed was true,
and might have been, for all we know?
Why silence him? Is it comforting
that there aren't any more posters now, accusing
those we know to be our enemies
of being our assassins?

Crazy he may be, and the Pentagon and the CIA
innocent as babes, but the poster's scream
of pain and paranoia is in its essence true—
there's been a war between man and microbe
from the beginning. And whether AIDS
is some kind of secret plot or not,
we must stand up with the poster man
and, as thousands die, refuse to be silenced,
scream from the rooftops,

AIDS IS GERM WARFARE AGAINST HUMANITY.

ONE MORE FOR THE QUILT

for Seth Allen

The last time we talked on a street corner
(we were always meeting on street corners)
you said you were on your way to the doctor,
there was something wrong with your throat—
it was the day rehearsals were starting
for the Broadway show, your big break.
> *Our friends are dying around us,*
> *and all of us left behind*
> *are awestruck with the horror of it.*
> *What, Lord, do you have in mind?*
> *Have mercy on us.*

That day, I took your hand in mine—
so warm and fleshy, full of high energy,
like the hands of a woman I worked for
who had cured herself of cancer. With those hands
I can hardly believe you couldn't
cure yourself of anything.
Though worried, you didn't in the least
have the look of someone about to die.
To the end, you were always ready for laughter,
> *even when you had a right to cry,*
> *Lord, have mercy on us.*

Sassy in print, Seth, your talent flowered anywhere—
on stage at La Mama you gave Caligula's speech
standing on the shoulders of two barechested hunks.
You never even wobbled—what balance,
defying gravity as you did in your life.
You were one of those who didn't need
the sexual revolution—you always went
all the way. No part of you was a prude.

The pleasure-loving, the boldest,
are disappearing from our midst,
And we who somehow still survive
can only beg, Don't take the best,
Lord, have mercy on us.

Strange, how much we talk about you, gone.
Even your dying didn't bring us down—
for you were one of those who added
to the store of gaiety on earth, the fun.
> *But even as memory tempers grief,*
> *the rest of us keep pondering*
> *that someone so full of life could die,*
> *while we, for the moment, remain alive—*
> *awestruck by your brief,*
> *brilliant flash across the sky:*

Lord, have mercy on us.

SUBSIDENCE

Lately, I have a feeling of the earth subsiding,
not everything going down gradually, though,
but uneven-like—a little here, a little there.
Sometimes more dramatic when a whole shelf of loam
gives way, tumbling down into the valley
to bury a village of screaming people—
I know that means big trouble—
and only if you're tremendously lucky
does a sink hole open or a forgotten, worked-out mine
below the streets collapse, and all the world
disappears in a night.

                        But mostly, these days, it feels
like a vast settling of the landscape,
green still, vivid green as that I saw
in Ireland once, where cow-browsed pastures
reach right to the world's edge,
and the loamy turf keeps breaking off and falling,
clod by grassy clod into the sea.

A New Stage, Sunday, March 22, 1992

Today, I have reached maturity.
It hits him while he is preparing dinner
and he rushes back to his desk to write it down:

Having reached my maturity, he writes,
I can summarize my path here . . .
He corrects this to,
Having reached my maturity
I am now able to look back and assess my life
with its erratic path of development.

He crosses out "erratic" to write,
"erotic" path of development.
He crosses out "look back," and writes,
I am now able to look forward
and assess my life.

As he shapes the hamburgers,
he thinks, *This is another*
creature's chopped-up flesh.
I'm not sure I can eat it.
But he does.
He goes on doing all his usual things.

He is joyful.
I have reached my full maturity
in 1992 at the age of 67, he repeats,
letting it sink in.
I am in my full powers.
It is an awesome thought.

He thanks his helpers:
Yoga, Grass, Poetry,

his friend Neil,
Music, the Carpets,
Sight.

He considers telling someone.
But how do you tell anyone about this?
It would sound crazy.

He thinks of how to celebrate,
mark the occasion with a ritual,
but he doesn't know how.
So he makes his ordinary life the celebration:
before bed, he smokes grass, does yoga
and transforms his body in the mirror,
until he experiences his penis fully,
and shoots.

Postscript, Day Two:
This is maturity,
not perfection.

AFTER CAVAFY

An old man in tears before The Muse:
In my whole life, he complains,
I have only written a few
slim books of poetry,
and gotten little attention for them.
I even see it in your pitiless eyes:
Why didn't I do more?

Perhaps they *were* too slim, too few.
But how to explain?
If I didn't try hard enough,
I don't even know why,
but always, other things
seemed to be more important.
Tell me, have I wasted my life,
as well as my talents?

Thus replies the statue:
Wipe your tears, old man.
You have taken a step
on the difficult ladder of poetry,
and even getting to the first rung
is an accomplishment the gods all praise.
Feel good about that, with my blessings,
for on this path,
there is no failure.

174

from STAND UP, FRIEND, WITH ME (1963)

HYDRA

This island whose name means water
Never had gods and temples as other Greek islands had;
It never was the home of monsters with ferocious heads
And maybe it wasn't even there.

But a few centuries ago
As though it had just risen from the sea
Men saw stones and pine trees on the slopes
And with the stones made houses and with the trees made ships.

And as naturally as fish swim
The ships went sailing;
And as naturally as the sun rises
The boys turned into heroes and sailed to war.

But the heroes were foolhardy as heroes are,
So although they were brave and did amazing things
The ships were sunk at last
And the handsome heroes lay on the ocean floor.

Wars over, fame won, the island settled down,
But with the trees all gone the soil blew away to sea;
The houses began to crumble,
And the island bleached in the sun to anonymity.

The name means water but now even the wells are drying
And no one expects the rock to grow trees again;
While the waters push gently on its shores
Waiting for the island to sink quietly back into the sea.

DONKEYS

They are not silent like workhorses
Who are happy or indifferent about the plow and wagon;
Donkeys don't submit like that
For they are sensitive
And cry continually under their burdens;
Yes, they are animals of sensibility
Even if they aren't intelligent enough
To count money or discuss religion.

Laugh if you will when they heehaw
But know that they are crying
When they make that noise that sounds like something
Between a squawking water pump and a foghorn.

And when I hear them sobbing
I suddenly notice their sweet eyes and ridiculous ears
And their naive bodies that look as though they never grew up
But stayed children, as in fact they are;
And being misunderstood as children are
They are forced to walk up mountains
With men and bundles on their backs.

Somehow I am glad that they do not submit without a protest
But as their masters are of the deafest
The wails are never heard.

I am sure that donkeys know what life should be
But, alas, they do not own their bodies;
And if they had their own way, I am sure
That they would sit in a field of flowers
Kissing each other, and maybe
They would even invite us to join them.

For they never let us forget that they know
(As everyone knows who stays as sweet as children)
That there is a far better way to spend time;
You can be sure of that when they stop in their tracks
And honk and honk and honk.

And if I tried to explain to them
Why work is not only necessary but good,
I am afraid that they would never understand
And kick me with their back legs
As commentary on my wisdom.

So they remain unhappy and sob
And their masters who are equally convinced of being right
Beat them and hear nothing.

UNWANTED

The poster with my picture on it
Is hanging on the bulletin board in the Post Office.

I stand by it hoping to be recognized
Posing first full face and then profile

But everyone passes by and I have to admit
The photograph was taken some years ago.

I was unwanted then and I'm unwanted now
Ah guess ah'll go up echo mountain and crah.

I wish someone would find my fingerprints somewhere
Maybe on a corpse and say, You're it.

Description: Male, or reasonably so
Complexion white, but not lily-white

Thirty-fivish, and looks it lately
Five-feet-nine and one-hundred-thirty pounds: no physique

Black hair going gray, hairline receding fast
What used to be curly, now fuzzy

Brown eyes starey under beetling brow
Mole on chin, probably will become a wen

It is perfectly obvious that he was not popular at school
No good at baseball, and wet his bed.

His aliases tell his history: Dumbbell, Good-for-nothing,
Jewboy, Fieldinsky, Skinny, Fierce Face, Greaseball, Sissy.

Warning: This man is not dangerous, answers to any name
Responds to love, don't call him or he will come.

180

Notes from a Slave Ship

It is necessary to wait until the boss's eyes are on you
Then simply put your work aside,
Slip a fresh piece of paper in the typewriter,
And start to write a poem.

Let their eyes boggle at your impudence;
The time for a poem is the moment of assertion,
The moment when you say I exist—
Nobody can buy my time absolutely.

Nobody can buy me even if I say, Yes I sell.
There I am sailing down the river,
Quite happy about the view of the passing towns,
When I find that I have jumped overboard.

There is always a long swim to freedom.
The worst of it is the terrible exhaustion
Alone in the water in the darkness,
The shore a fading memory and the direction lost.

POEM FOR THE LEFT HAND

Cancer strikes and I lose my left hand:
My whole life has to be reorganized
Since I can no longer earn my living as a typist.
I am now one of the obviously crippled
Although to tell the truth
I have been one of them for as long as I can remember,
And all those years I was aware
That I was in the state of cancer if not cancerous yet.
My concern was laughed at.

Life is simpler now; no one will dream
Of looking further than my handless arm
For my deformity; it will be a hook to hang my troubles on,
For of course I shall wear a hook in its place
Rather than one of those prosthetic appliances,
And I shall join the ranks of other men
Who blame their troubles on similar unalterable situations
Such as the wife, or automation (the machine replacing the hand),
And they are right. Something is wrong with people
Who say it's me that's wrong, my nature needs changing.
Our nature is God's various will
And each oddity precious for the evolving animal kingdom.

Now that I am back to hunt and peck
I thank God for granting me this reprieve
From that endless unraveling of my nature.
Knots are too difficult for one hand to be bothered with:
Now I cut them through and laugh for the liberation.

A Bill to My Father

I am typing up bills for a firm to be sent to their clients.
It occurs to me that firms are sending bills to my father
Who has that way an identity I do not often realize.
He is a person who buys, owes, and pays.
Not papa like he is to me.
His creditors reproach him for not paying on time
With a bill marked "Please Remit."
I reproach him for never having shown his love for me
But only his disapproval.
He has a debt to me too
Although I have long since ceased asking him to come across;
He does not know how and so I do without it.
But in this impersonal world of business
He can be communicated with:
With absolute assurance of being paid
The boss writes "Send me my money"
And my father sends it.

THE TELEPHONE

My happiness depends on an electric appliance
And I do not mind giving it so much credit
With life in this city being what it is
Each person separated from friends
By a tangle of subways and buses
Yes my telephone is my joy
It tells me that I am in the world and wanted
It rings and I am alerted to love or gossip
I go comb my hair which begins to sparkle
Without it I was like a bear in a cave
Drowsing through a shadowy winter
It rings and spring has come
I stretch and amble out into the sunshine
Hungry again as I pick up the receiver
For the human voice and the good news of friends

A JOURNEY

When he got up that morning everything was different:
He enjoyed the bright spring day
But he did not realize it exactly, he just enjoyed it.

And walking down the street to the railroad station
Past magnolia trees with dying flowers like old socks
It was a long time since he had breathed so simply.

Tears filled his eyes and it felt good
But he held them back
Because men didn't walk around crying in that town.

And waiting on the platform at the station
The fear came over him of something terrible about to happen:
The train was late and he recited the alphabet to keep hold.

And in its time it came screeching in
And as it went on making its usual stops,
People coming and going, telephone poles passing,

He hid his head behind a newspaper
No longer able to hold back the sobs, and willed his eyes
To follow the rational weavings of the seat fabric.

He didn't do anything violent as he had imagined.
He cried for a long time, but when he finally quieted down
A place in him that had been closed like a fist was open,

And at the end of the ride he stood up and got off that train:
And through the streets and in all the places he lived in later on
He walked, himself at last, a man among men,
With such radiance that everyone looked up and wondered.

PROLOGUE

Look, friend, at this universe
With its spiral clusters of stars
Flying out all over space
Like bedsprings suddenly busting free;
And in this galaxy, the sun
Fissioning itself away,
Surrounded by planets, prominent in their dignity,
And bits and pieces running wild;
And this middling planet
With a lone moon circling round it.

Look, friend, through the fog of gases at this world
With its skin of earth and rock, water and ice,
With various creatures and rooted things;
And up from the bulging waistline
To this land of concrete towers,
Its roads swarming like a hive cut open,
Offshore to this island, long and fishshaped,
Its mouth to a metropolis,
And in its belly, this village,
A gathering of families at a crossways,
And in this house, upstairs and through the wide open door
Of the front bedroom with a window on the world,
Look, friend, at me.

CHOPIN

Chopin is such a great composer
I can even write poetry while his music is on the radio
Which is unusual for me.
He makes my fingers nimble like ballerinas on the keys.
He says, Let's go to town slambang on the whole goddam
              machine.

I love you Chopin in spite of the million fingers
Of little girls with long bobbing curls
Practicing your notes during daylight hours
But mostly three to five after school.
You set the hands of the children of the world
Grubbing at the keyboard
Like Pavlova put them on their wobbly toes.

I love you Chopin in spite of Merle Oberon
Although that was a pretty good movie where sweet Paul Muni
Still had two good eyes to see you were a genius.
I liked how he made you fight for Polish nationalism
That dead duck with two heads;
But of course really he was urging you
Not to turn over the Jews to the Germans
And your fingers flew like mad to save them,
But you couldn't save them since piano playing
Never saves anyone except the player if he's cute besides
(Like Van Cliburn walking through the iron curtain).
Anyway when my mother was a girl in Poland
It had become a nation already, a nation of Jew-haters
So it couldn't have been the result of your gorgeous music
Which clearly says, Love the Jews.

Chopin, my soul,
Don't listen to those critics with their dried-up eyes;

They don't like me either, my poems embarrass them.
You are too good for them
So if they want to snub you, let them,
Let them miss out on all the fun in life
Like making love and dancing about and being Mediterranean,
Still acting silly and uncynical like sixteen,
Like promising to love forever and ever and ever, and doing it.

SONNY HUGG AND THE PORCUPINE

This baby porcupine squeezing into a crevice of rock
Could be hauled out into the open,
poked with a stick, and otherwise toyed with,
But cute as he was he couldn't be kissed.

Love rose tender in the heart of Sonny Hugg
And he dreamed impossible dreams.
But all those bristles! His mind twisted and turned
To find a workable solution.

To hug this improbable child was important to him,
The child willing or no, and who could say it wasn't willing.
Maybe the Gillette, the garden shears . . . No, without those spurs
This creature would be unlovable as a rat.

Sonny was versatile but this defeated him.
He faced reality. A porcupine for a lover?
Alas, he would have to settle for those creations
Not quite as darling but with bodies good for hugging.

GRAFFITI

Blessings on all the kids who improve the signs in the subways:
They put a beard on the fashionable lady selling soap,
Fix up her flat chest with the boobies of a chorus girl,
And though her hips be wrapped like a mummy
They draw a hairy cunt where she should have one.

The bathing beauty who looks pleased
With the enormous prick in her mouth, declares
"Eat hair pie; it's better than cornflakes."
And the little boy in the Tarzan suit eating white bread
Now has a fine pair of balls to crow about.

And as often as you wash the walls and put up your posters,
When you go back to the caged booth to deal out change
The bright-eyed kids will come with grubby hands.
Even if you watch, you cannot watch them all the time,
And while you are dreaming, if you have dreams anymore,

A boy and girl are giggling behind an iron pillar;
And although the train pulls in and takes them on their way
Into a winter that will freeze them forever,
They leave behind a wall scrawled all over with flowers
That shoot great drops of gism through the sky.

A New Cycle

My father buying me the bicycle that time
Was an unusual thing for him to do.
He believed that a parent's duty meant the necessities:
Food, clothing, shelter, and music lessons.

I had hardly dared to ask him for it
And I didn't believe he really meant to buy me one
Until I saw him take out the money and hand it over—
Eight dollars secondhand, but newly painted, and good rubber.

And I couldn't thank him, a hug was out of the question with us,
So I just got up on it and rode a ways shakily
And then I made him ride it—
He didn't even know he was supposed to say it was a good bike.

I rode off on it into a new life, paper route, pocket money,
Dances in other towns where the girls found me attractive,
And sexual adventures that would have made my father's hair
Stand up in horror had he known.

Daddy I can thank you now for the bike you gave me
Which meant more to me than you knew, or could have stood to
          know.
I rode away to everywhere it could take me, until finally
It took me to this nowhere, this noplace I am now.

I just passed my thirty-fifth birthday,
The end of a seven-year cycle and the beginning of a new one,
And sure enough I woke up the first day quite empty,
Everything over, with nothing to do and no ideas for the future.

Daddy whom I now can hug and kiss
Who gives me money when I ask,

What shall I do with this life you gave me
That cannot be junked like a bicycle when it wears out?

Is it utterly ridiculous for a man thirty-five years old and graying
To sit in his father's lap and ask for a bike? Even if he needs one?
Whom shall he ask if not his father?
Daddy, darling Daddy, please buy me a bicycle.

THE CHARMED POOL

At the charmed pool swarming with the lower forms of life,
The flying, the crawling, the swimming, and the stationary,
Prince Charming looked around and wondered
Which of these creatures was the Princess
Who, the story said, was victim of a witch's curse
And waited for his kiss to reappear.

He was willing to try this kissing game
Even if a snake or a stone wasn't his idea of a good time.
To begin he chose a green frog with a gummy eye
And waded after it into the water feeling ridiculous
But with a sense of fulfilling prophecy.
Oh prince, prince, will you never grow up?

He caught the amphibian in his hand
And planted a kiss where he guessed its mouth was
And Prince Foolish, still pimpled from self-abuse,
Swooning with the same old admiration,
Was in his arms. He dropped him flat.
This magic can be an odd occupation.

He sat about kissing all the creatures
Like the game of knock-knock-who's-there:
A dragonfly turned into Jack the Jew-Killer,
A mushroom into Miss Venom of the grammar school,
And soon there were lots of unpleasant people sitting around.
That witch had excellent taste in whom to banish.

Finally from a stone he got a princess,
Not his Princess to be sure, but the orphan princess,
With a calculated tear running down her nose
And crossed eyes that said, "Pity me."

He had; until he found her in the scullery with his uncle,
Praying at the head and sinning at the tail.

This had gone far enough; the Princess obviously wasn't there.
He took off his Prince costume
Revealing a quite attractive but ordinary young man
Who no longer knew what to do or where to go.
According to the story he found his princess at last
But, reader, do you really think he did?

This charming Prince who thought life had a happy ending,
I don't like to leave him like that naked by the pool,
The legend on the ground like a heap of worn-out clothing.
But if I said anything definite it would just be made up.
When a man tries the charmed pool and fails
What can he do if he doesn't die of it?

Is he wandering about the forest waiting to be found?
By whom? For what? He'll be a heap of bones by then.
Did he find the road back to where he came from?
And learn like us to live from day to day
Eating what's to eat and making love with what's available?
And did he ever fall in love again?

ODE TO FIDEL CASTRO

I.

O Boy God, Muse of Poets
Come sit on my shoulder while I write
Cuddle up and fill my poem with love
And even while I fly on billows of inspiration
Don't forget to tickle me now and then
For I am going to write on World Issues
Which demands laughter where we most believe.

Also, My Cute One, don't let me take a heroic pose
And act as though I know it all
Guard me from Poet's Head that dread disease
Where the words ring like gongs and meaning goes out the
            window
Remind me of the human size of truth
Whenever I spout a big, ripe absolute
(Oh why did you let the architects of our capital city
Design it for giants
So that a man just has to take a short walk and look about
For exhaustion to set in immediately)
Please, Sweet Seeker, don't discourage me from contradicting
            myself
But make everything sound like life, like people we like
And most of all give me strength not to lay aside this poem
Like so many others in the pile by my typewriter
But to write the whole thing from beginning to end
O Perfection, the way it wants to go.

II.

My subject, Dear Muse, is Fidel Castro
Rebellissimo and darling of the Spanish-American lower classes
A general who adopted for his uniform

The work clothes of the buck private and the beard of the saints
A man fit for ruling a great nation
But who only has an island.

Irene, the beautiful Cuban, has his picture over her bed
Between Rudulph Valentino and the Blessed Virgin —
He stands large and flabby between the perfect body and the
          purest soul
Doves on his shoulders, on his open hands
And one dove for crown standing on his head —
He is not afraid of birdshit, his face is radiant.

Someday Hollywood will make a movie biography of his life
Starring the spreading Marlon Brando
They'll invent a great love on his way up, a blonde with a large
          crucifix
Whom he loses along with his idealism, and once at the top
A great passion, a dark whore with large breasts, to drag him
          down.
In real life his romance is with his people and his role
Otherwise his sex life is normal for his age and position.

Fidel, Fidel, Fidel . . .
I am in love with the spotlight myself
And would like the crowds to chant my name
Which has the same letters as yours but rearranged
Where is my island Where my people
What am I doing on this continent Where is my crown
Where did everyone go that used to call me king
And light up like votive candles when I smiled?
(I have given them all up for you sweet youth my muse
Be truly mine.)

Am I like Goethe who kept faith in Napoleon
Long after the rest of the world had given him up
For tyrant and the betrayer of the revolution?
If Napoleon was like Tolstoy writing a novel
Organizing a vast army of plots and themes
Then Castro is like a poet writing an ode

(Alas that poets should be rulers—
Revise that line, cut that stanza, lop off that phrase)
Paredon! Paredon!

What he did was kick out the bad men and good riddance Batista
What he is doing . . . Well, what he is trying to do is . . .
(Muse, why don't you help me with this,
Are you scared of socialist experiment?)
One thing he is doing is upsetting a lot of people
Our papers are full of stories that make him out a devil
And you a fool if you like him
But they are against me too even if they don't know I exist
So let's shake Fidel
(The hand that exists shakes the hand that doesn't)
My Fidel Castro, Star of Cuba.

III.

The Hotel Teresa in Harlem is a dumpy landmark in a slum
But when Fidel Castro went there to stay
And when Nikita Khrushchev went up and hugged and kissed
        him for being Mr. Wonderful
Right out in public (they get away with it those foreigners)
Then Harlem became the capital of the world
And the true home of the united nations.

That whole bunch sitting around the hotel like in bivouac roasting
        chickens
And all those Negroes looking at them bug-eyed—
Nobody that great ever came up there before to stay.
Of course plenty of people that great came out of Harlem
Like Jimmy Baldwin, not to mention those jazz people we all love
But the Colored that came out of Harlem like roman candles
You don't catch them going back there like a Fourth of July
        parade.
Now Cuba and Russia have gone to Harlem
And found it a good place for loving—
That Harlem, full of rats chewing off babies' arms

And social workers trying to keep the whole place from exploding
I used to have friends up there
When I went to visit them if I passed a mirror
My whiteness would surprise me
The mind takes on darkness of skin so easily
(Of course being a Jew I'm not exactly white)
It is that easy to turn black
And then have to be in that awful boat the Negroes are in
Although it's pretty lousy being white
And having that black hatred turned on you.

What after all can a white man say but, I'm ashamed
Hey fellas I'm sorry . . .
Unless you are President and then you have your golden
        opportunity.
Perhaps the only thing to do is look upon each other
As two men look when they meet solitary in the deep woods
Come black man let us jerk off together
Like boys do to get to know each other.

Well just like others who have escaped ghettos I don't go to
       Harlem anymore
I don't like to see the trapped whom I can't set free
But when I see the big front-page photos of Castro and
       Khrushchev hugging in Harlem
A widescreen spectacle with supermen in totalscope embrace, and
       in color yet
I sit back and dig it all the way.

IV.

BOMBS GOING OFF ALL OVER HAVANA
In Rockefeller Center the Cuban Tourist Office is closed
And across the skating rink men are putting up
The world's largest Christmas tree which will never be Christian
Even if you cut it down, make it stand on cement, decorate it
       with balls
It will still scream for the forest, like a wild animal

Like the gods who love freedom and topple to the saws of
    commerce
The gods who frighten us half to death in our dreams with their
    doings
And disappear when we need them most, awake.

By the time you see this, Fidel, you might not even exist anymore
My government is merciless and even now
The machine to destroy you is moving into action
The chances are you won't last long
Well so long pal it was nice knowing you
I can't go around with a broken heart all my life
After I got over the fall of the Spanish Republic
I guess I can get over anything
My job is just to survive.
But I wish you well Fidel Castro
And if you do succeed in making that island
The tropic paradise God meant it to be
I'll be the first to cheer and come for a free visit if invited.

So you're not perfect, poets don't look for perfect
It's your spirit we love and the glamour of your style
I hope someday the cameras of the world
Are turned on you and me in some spot like Harlem
And then you'll get a kiss that will make Khrushchev's be
    forgotten
A kiss of the poet, that will make you truly good
The way you meant to be.

Tulips and Addresses

The Museum of Modern Art on West Fifty-third Street
Is interested only in the flower not the bulb:
After the Dutch tulips finished blooming in the garden last year
They pulled them up and threw them away—that place has no
       heart.
Some fortunately were rescued and came into my possession.

I kept them all winter in a paper bag from the A & P
At first where I was living then on the West Side
Until the next-door tribe of Murphies drove me out with rock
      and roll,
Then at Thompson Street in the Village where overhead
A girl and her lover tromped around all night on each other.

And that wasn't the end of it: I shlepped those bulbs around
For two months from place to place looking for a home,
All that winter, moving . . . Oy—although this was nothing new
      for me
Coming as I do from a wandering race,
And life with its ten plagues making me even more Jewish.

Now I am living on Abingdon Square, not the Ritz exactly, but a
      place
And I have planted the tulips in my window box:
Please God make them come up, so that everyone who passes by
Will know I'm here, at least long enough to catch my breath,
When they see the bright red beautiful flowers in my window.

THE SLEEPER

When I was the sissy of the block who nobody wanted on their
          team
Sonny Hugg persisted in believing that my small size was an asset
Not the liability and curse I felt it was
And he saw a use for my swift feet with which I ran away from
          fights.

He kept putting me into complicated football plays
Which would have been spectacular if they worked:
For instance, me getting clear in front and him shooting the ball
          over—
Or the sensation of the block, the Sleeper Play
In which I would lie down on the sidelines near the goal
As though resting and out of action, until the scrimmage began
And I would step onto the field, receive the long throw
And to the astonishment of all the tough guys in the world
Step over the goal line for a touchdown.

That was the theory anyway. In practice
I had the fatal flaw of not being able to catch
And usually had my fingers bent back and the breath knocked out
          of me
So the plays always failed, but Sonny kept on trying
Until he grew up out of my world into the glamorous
Varsity crowd, the popular kids of Lynbrook High.

But I will always have this to thank him for:
That when I look back on childhood
(That four psychiatrists haven't been able to help me bear the
          thought of)
There is not much to be glad for
Besides his foolish and delicious faith
That, with all my oddities, there was a place in the world for me
If only he could find the special role.

AT THE CONEY ISLAND AQUARIUM: AN ODE FOR OOKIE, THE OLDER WALRUS CHILD, OR THE SIBLING RIVAL

Do not worry, sweet little walrus, about the superior cuteness
Of those two new babies they brought to share your pool.

You keep pushing the twins out of the way
More concerned about keeping them from getting attention
Than having your own scrub-brush nose whiskers rubbed
So that no one gets the chance to give you
The endless hugs and kisses you deserve.

It is impossible of course to be more popular than twins
So finally you sink to the bottom and play dead
Hoping our hearts break—mine does anyway
And the Keeper watches anxiously, so you see it works.
But how long can you sit at the bottom of the water
When lungs cry for air and the heart for love?

No, Ookie, don't seek indiscriminate love from the many
As those two simple-minded children do
Who have not yet met with heartbreak (although they will),
But leap the railing right into my arms
And squirm there fishily always, Ookie, mine alone.

202

The Garden

The plants on the window ledge are all growing well
Except the avocado which is dying

The grapefruit seeds from breakfast came up
And the watermelon are sprouting all over the window box

The mango practically exploded it looked so pregnant
Cherry, peach, apple and plum trees flourish

The potato eyes threw up weird white shoots
And the birdseed grew a good crop of ragweed

We have formed a colony in a strange land
Planting our seeds and making ourselves at home

I look around, everything in order
The implements of living stacked

Fishes in the stream blowing bubbles like kisses
Wild cats to drag yowling from the woods

Trees to hug and roots to dig
A young horse to play around with

It is a beautiful place to have the run of
When a sweet creature of your own brings all of it to you.

from Variety Photoplays (1967)

FRANKENSTEIN

The monster has escaped from the dungeon
where he was kept by the Baron,
who made him with knobs sticking out from each side of his
            neck
where the head was attached to the body
and stitching all over
where parts of cadavers were sewed together.

He is pursued by the ignorant villagers,
who think he is evil and dangerous because he is ugly
and makes ugly noises.
They wave firebrands at him and cudgels and rakes,
but he escapes and comes to the thatched cottage
of an old blind man playing on the violin Mendelssohn's "Spring
            Song."

Hearing him approach, the blind man welcomes him:
"Come in, my friend," and takes him by the arm.
"You must be weary," and sits him down inside the house.
For the blind man has long dreamed of having a friend
to share his lonely life.

The monster has never known kindness — the Baron was cruel —
but somehow he is able to accept it now,
and he really has no instincts to harm the old man,
for in spite of his awful looks he has a tender heart:
Who knows what cadaver that part of him came from?

The old man seats him at table, offers him bread,
and says, "Eat, my friend." The monster
rears back roaring in terror.
"No, my friend, it is good. Eat — gooood"
and the old man shows him how to eat,

and reassured, the monster eats
and says, "Eat—gooood,"
trying out the words and finding them good too.

The old man offers him a glass of wine,
"Drink, my friend. Drink—goood."
The monster drinks, slurping horribly, and says,
"Drink—goood," in his deep nutty voice
and smiles maybe for the first time in his life.

Then the blind man puts a cigar in the monster's mouth
and lights a large wooden match that flares up in his face.
The monster, remembering the torches of the villagers,
recoils, grunting in terror.
"No, my friend, smoke—goood,"
and the old man demonstrates with his own cigar.
The monster takes a tentative puff
and smiles hugely, saying, "Smoke—goood,"
and sits back like a banker, grunting and puffing.

Now the old man plays Mendelssohn's "Spring Song" on the
                violin
while tears come into our dear monster's eyes
as he thinks of the stones of the mob, the pleasures of mealtime,
the magic new words he has learned
and above all of the friend he has found.

It is just as well that he is unaware—
being simple enough to believe only in the present—
that the mob will find him and pursue him
for the rest of his short unnatural life,
until trapped at the whirlpool's edge
he plunges to his death.

CURSE OF THE CAT WOMAN

It sometimes happens
that the woman you meet and fall in love with
is of that strange Transylvanian people
with an affinity for cats.

You take her to a restaurant, say, or a show,
on an ordinary date, being attracted
by the glitter in her slitty eyes and her catlike walk,
and afterwards of course you take her in your arms
and she turns into a black panther
and bites you to death.

Or perhaps you are saved in the nick of time
and she is tormented by the knowledge of her tendency:
that she daren't hug a man
unless she wants to risk clawing him up.

This puts you both in a difficult position—
panting lovers who are prevented from touching
not by bars but by circumstance:
you have terrible fights and say cruel things
for having the hots does not give you a sweet temper.

One night you are walking down a dark street
and hear the pad-pad of a panther following you,
but when you turn around there are only shadows,
or perhaps one shadow too many.

You approach, calling, "Who's there?"
and it leaps on you.
Luckily you have brought along your sword
and you stab it to death.

And before your eyes it turns into the woman you love,
her breast impaled on your sword,
her mouth dribbling blood saying she loved you
but couldn't help her tendency.

So death released her from the curse at last,
and you knew from the angelic smile on her dead face
that in spite of a life the devil owned,
love had won, and heaven pardoned her.

WHATEVER HAPPENED TO MAY CASPAR?

A Narration for an Animated Cartoon

What happens to old movie stars,
those faded queens of stage and screen?
They move into hotels off Times Square maybe
where they live among their souvenirs,
near the lights, the people, the premières
that no longer know them—
funny old ladies with hair a pink frizz,
salvaging old costumes for street clothes.

Does anyone remember May Caspar now?
She was all the rage in thirty-three
when she starred in *May Morning* with Ronald Peale,
in which she played a simple country girl
and he a prince who lost his heart among the apple blossoms.

Now thirty years later (that makes her about sixty, at least),
what does she see when she sits down to her vanity table
with its clutter of lotions?
Does she stare at the blur in the mirror
and remember how young she was in that movie,
how pure and fragile?
Before she puts on her glasses
she takes a swig out of a large perfume bottle,
and goes about painting a kewpie doll over the wreck of her face:
Somehow it always comes out crooked.

Later, after her disastrous marriage to Nick Kinsella
and the divorce and the operations
(they say he beat her up horribly),
after she got back her looks,
she played *femme fatale* roles on divans with heavy eye makeup.

Remember *A Woman's Eyes,* with Ivan Carlovan,
in which May was the toast of Vienna
until the love of her prince turned to hate
when he discovered a stableboy was her lover
and she had to flee through snowdrifts in a sleigh
standing up behind the horses singing:
>   *The heart will find a way*
but ending up in a waterfront bar in Marseilles
singing with an accordion:
>   *A woman's eyes are pools of sin*
>   *Don't look too long, they'll lure you in.*
There were dozens of suicides to her record of that song.

Then came her greatest hit, *The Downward Path,*
in which she played a mature star
who fell in love with a young actor,
but he only used her to make it to the top
while she went downhill fast and ended in the gutter
selling flowers by the stage door
as he came out with the ingénue on his arm,
and stepped into the waiting limousine.
How her beautiful eyes shone in that scene!
You knew she held no grudge, but loved him still
as she sang after him:
>   *Go, beautiful youth,*
>   *forget me now, for I am old.*
>   *Enjoy your fame as I did mine.*
For that, America forgave her everything,
her parade of unsuitable husbands,
her drunken brawls in restaurants.
She was darling May Caspar, for a few years anyway
(her career lasted only three more years),
then she faded away.

Now forgotten, she is that funny old lady
living shabbily on a dwindling income
in a Times Square hotel, once genteel,
now full of call girls and Kansas tourists.
It gets harder and harder to pay the bills.

Back rent mounts up. Room service is cut off.
She lives on hot dogs. Her fate looks grim.
She is about to be put out in the street
with her souvenirs and wardrobe
for the winter wind to blow away,
plumes and bits of fur and photographs and dried corsages,
and she skittering after them down the streets.

But wait, here comes a late rider:
a message from the Museum of Modern Art!
They are planning a May Caspar revival
and she is wanted to appear "in person," like the old days.
May Caspar movies stamped Authentic American Art.
She is proclaimed A Great Actress.
May Caspar Called Back to Hollywood to Make Film.
But first she goes to Last Chance,
exclusive beauty resort in Death Valley,
where they go to work on her
with hormones, vitamins, embryo implants, and surgery.

When she shows up in Hollywood her beauty is restored.
Thirty years of ravagement have been erased:
there is not a wrinkle.
Of course her strength is not what it was —
two men have to hold her up,
but she is a great trouper and the show will go on.
Today they are filming her big scene on the divan, her trademark:
Lights, Camera, Action: May Caspar acts again!

Anyway she tries, but the effort is too much for her —
the hot lights, the excitement,
her skin held taut by invisible clips,
her heart stimulated with drugs,
her head sweating under the wig,
every bit of her is held together with string and sealing wax.
"Okay Miss Caspar, give it all you've got."
The camera moves in inexorably for the closeup.
She tries desperately to think young, to hold everything up.

Those merciless lights!
Too late, it all collapses.

Goodbye May Caspar.
We loved you
in the way we love—
faithlessly.
Or are we, growing older,
ready to remember again
our great loves
of yesteryear
and go search for them
where we lost sight of them
in those shabby place,
close to the brightest
lights
that cast the deepest
shadow?

The Bride of Frankenstein

The Baron has decided to mate the monster,
to breed him perhaps,
in the interests of pure science, his only god.

So he goes up into his laboratory
which he has built in the tower of the castle
to be as near the interplanetary forces as possible,
and puts together the prettiest monster-woman you ever saw
with a body like a pin-up girl
and hardly any stitching at all
where he sewed on the head of a raped and murdered beauty
        queen.

He sets his liquids burping, and coils blinking and buzzing,
and waits for an electric storm to send through the equipment
the spark vital for life.
The storm breaks over the castle
and the equipment really goes crazy
like a kitchen full of modern appliances
as the lightning juice starts oozing right into that pretty corpse.

He goes to get the monster
so he will be right there when she opens her eyes,
for she might fall in love with the first thing she sees as ducklings
        do.
That monster is already straining at his chains and slurping,
ready to go right to it:
he has been well prepared for coupling
by his pinching leering keeper, who's been saying for weeks,
"Ya gonna get a little nookie, kid,"
or "How do you go for some poontang, baby?"
All the evil in him is focused on this one thing now
as he is led into her very presence.

She awakens slowly,
she bats her eyes,
she gets up out of the equipment,
and finally she stands in all her seamed glory,
a monster princess with a hairdo like a fright wig,
lightning flashing in the background
like a halo and a wedding veil,
like a photographer snapping pictures of great moments.

She stands and stares with her electric eyes,
beginning to understand that in this life too
she was just another body to be raped.
The monster is ready to go:
he roars with joy at the sight of her,
so they let him loose and he goes right for those knockers.
And she starts screaming to break your heart
and you realize that she was just born:
in spite of her big tits she was just a baby.

But her instincts are right—
rather death than that green slobber:
she jumps off the parapet.
And then the monster's sex drive goes wild.
Thwarted, it turns to violence, demonstrating sublimation crudely;
and he wrecks the lab, those burping acids and buzzing coils,
overturning the control panel so the equipment goes off like a
          bomb,
the stone castle crumbling and crashing in the storm,
destroying them all . . . perhaps.

Perhaps somehow the Baron got out of that wreckage of his
          dreams
with his evil intact, if not his good looks,
and more wicked than ever went on with his thrilling career.
And perhaps even the monster lived
to roam the earth, his desire still ungratified;
and lovers out walking in shadowy and deserted places
will see his shape loom up over them, their doom—

and children sleeping in their beds
will wake up in the dark night screaming
as his hideous body grabs them.

THE LIFE OF JOAN CRAWFORD

for Barbara Barry

She was a working girl from a small town
but the town wasn't so small
that it didn't have a railroad track
dividing the right side from the wrong side.
On the right side was the Hill
where the swells lived in big houses,
and on the wrong side, the Hollow where the proletariat
spent their greasy and unrewarding lives.
(For in those days the American town
was a living demonstration of Marxist theory.)

Joan of course lived in the Hollow
in one of those shacks with sagging porches
the mill put up rows of for the workers.
Her father, Tim Crawford, was the town drunk
living on relief and odd jobs
ever since the mines closed down when Joan was a baby.
He had been waiting for them to reopen for twenty years.
Joan never knew what had happened to her mother:
Joan's birth, her mother's disappearance or death, the mine's
                    closing,
that was in a time of violence no one would discuss.
Just mention it and her father went on a binge,
not that he was ever sober.

She sighed, and went off to work in the five-and ten
wearing her made-over dress with little washable collar and cuffs.
Even with her prole accent and the cheap bag and shoes
she was a good looker.
Men used to come by in their flashy suits and big cigars,
call her tootsie and ask for a date,
but she knew a poor girl didn't stand a chance with them.

She wasn't one of those innocents
who think a guy loves you if he gets a hard-on.
Yet she wouldn't go with any of the boys from the Hollow either
because with them the future was sleazy with kids
and the ruin of her figure before she was thirty—
and no fun after the honeymoon
except the Friday-night fight
when he would come home stinking, having drunk up the
            paycheck
and beat her black and blue
when she threw the stack of overdue bills at him—
and then screw her viciously on the dining-room table.
Some fun.
That was life in the Hollow and she wasn't having any.
She had turned down a job working in the mill
where the pay was better but life closed like a trap on you
and chose the more ladylike job at the five-and-ten
where people called her Miss and she could pose genteely
behind the Tangee cosmetic display and the ribbon counter.
For Joan had the makings of a lady
if she could ever get some dough to fix herself up with
and a speech teacher to correct her dreadful accent.

But Nature had its way with Joan at last:
Spring came and handsome John Wainrich
(of the best family in town—they owned everything,
the five-and-dime, the shut mines, and the mill),
John Wainrich came in one day to collect the receipts or
            something
and found a million-dollar baby in his own five-and-ten-cents
            store.
Well Joan fell hard
and went out with him in his big car
and of course in the moonlight she let him have his way with her.
She used to meet him on the sly
when he could get away from the country club
and the milk-white debutante he was engaged to,
and they would drive out to roadhouses
where he wouldn't be seen by his swell friends.

Joan had pride,
but what is a woman's pride when she's in love.
What it came to, a few months later,
was that she got pregnant,
and just as she was about to break the good news,
he told her he was going to be married
and would have to stop seeing her until after the wedding,
that it was just a marriage of convenience
and wouldn't make any difference to them.
So she couldn't tell him then, she would have died first.
My great love, she muttered sarcastically,
he didn't even use a scum-bag.
And she went off to the city
where she got a job as receptionist in an office.
Her boss, Mr. Harris, was an older but dignified man
with a wife at home on Park Avenue, the victim of neurosis and
        wealth—
with all that money she could buy neither health nor happiness.
Joan used to listen to Mr. Harris's troubles
when she brought him his alka-seltzer mornings.
And when she was promoted to secretary, they would have dinner
        out
and she'd advise him on business,
she being a girl with a good head on her shoulders.

In Mr. Harris's company she saw the world and learned fast.
She lost her small-town look and learned to dress,
wearing hat and gloves, to fluff out her hair
and drink vermouth cocktails.
And while retaining the colorful idiom of the Hollow,
her grammar improved and her voice lost its nasal whine.
Joan was a knockout in every way
from honest eyes and square shoulders
to the narrow hips of a tango dancer.

Nothing showed yet in the baby department.
At night Joan looked critically at herself in the mirror:
not a bulge, but baby was in there all right,
and her eyes went bitter as she thought of its father—

her great love, hmph.
"Well young feller, at least we'll have each other.
But I'd better be making preparations.
A working girl can't leave things to the caterer."

Then her boss proposed: He'd divorce his wife and marry her.
"Gee Mr. Harris, I think you're swell but I can't.
There is a real big favor you could do for me, though,"
and she told him how she gave her all for love
and her lover turned out to be a louse.
So Mr. Harris set her up in a little flat until the baby came.
He didn't make any demands on her or anything,
not yet anyway: it was sort of a promissory note
to be paid off later when she grew to love him out of gratitude.

But her ex-lover, John Wainrich, came to town
with his new wedding ring on, and tracked her down;
and misunderstanding the arrangement, called her a few names,
but swore she was his and he'd never give her up.
Joan still loved him but had the courage
to flee to a cheap hotel.
She got a job as dance-hall hostess, dime-a-dance,
six months pregnant, but with a brave smile
as the customers stepped on her toes.
They found her a good joe and a willing ear
as they told her their troubles
while rubbing off against her to a slow foxtrot.
One of her customers, impressed by her dancing,
got her to enter a dance marathon with him for prize money —
she needed that dough for the little stranger —
but the strain was too much for her,
marathon-dancing in her seventh month!

She came to on a hospital bed
with no makeup on and a white cloth over her forehead like a nun
to see her griddle-faced father looking down on her,
his mouth boozy as ever, but in his heart
vowing to go on the wagon if God would spare her life:
"Come home with me, Joanie, I'll take care of you."

"And baby too, Papa?"
"Didn't they tell you, Joanie? The baby . . ."
"Oh no . . ."
And tears of mourning still in her eyes
she went back to the Hollow and kept house for her father.

She had two visits shortly after returning home:
First, John's pale bride came by, big with child,
neglect driving her to seek out her rival.
When she saw Joan so sweet and good
instead of some tramp homewrecker type,
she burst into tears and confessed she knew John didn't love her
but hoped he would when the baby was born, his heir.
The bitterness in Joan's heart turned to pity—
weren't they both women who had suffered?—
so she forgave her and they wept together:
Joan never could resist being a pal.

The other visit was from old Mr. Wainrich, John's father.
(Never had the Hollow seen so many long cars drive through.)
The old capitalist had a confession to make:
"When I saw you at the window watering the geraniums
I could have sworn you were your mother."
"You knew my mother, Mr. Wainrich?" asked Joan astonished.
"Yes. Bette wasn't like the other women in the Hollow.
She was a Davis you know. Her parents
had been plantation people down in Georgia
and even if they did end up here in the Hollow
she never forgot that she was a thoroughbred."
"Are you trying to tell me that you loved my mother?" Joan
              gasped.

"Yes, I loved her, but the heir to an industrial empire
isn't free to marry whom he chooses,
so my family chose an appropriate bride for me.
At that time I was running our coal mines here,
where your father worked.
He was the biggest and toughest man in the Hollow
so naturally he was spokesman for the boys.

He had loved your mother for years
but she knew what it meant for a woman to marry a miner
and live in constant fear of a cave-in.
And she hated his coarse language and crude manners: she was a
	lady.
And besides, she loved me.
But when I broke the news of my engagement to her
(I explained it was just a marriage of convenience
and it wouldn't make any difference to us)
she married Tim just to spite me.
But it wasn't enough for her: right on my wedding day
she got Tim Crawford to call the men out on strike,
and, with violence surging around the Hill,
I had the biggest wedding ever seen in these parts.
I was coal and my bride was steel: what a merger!
The President came, and there were reporters from Chicago,
and your mother, already big with child, leading the picket line.

That strike went on for months, and you were born in the middle
	of it.
But we couldn't go on apart, your mother and I.
We knew we were sinners, but we managed to meet on the sly,
although the strike had turned the town into a battlefield
and we belonged to opposing armies.
Finally we decided to run away together, but just at that time
a load of scabs I was importing to work the mines arrived,
and there was a tremendous battle between them and the miners,
led by Tim Crawford of course.
The miners had lead pipes and dynamite,
but we had the National Guard in full battle dress.
Your mother and I, eloping, got caught in the middle
and took refuge in a deserted mine;
and I don't know which side did it, but a stick of dynamite
was thrown down the shaft, and your mother
was buried by a ton of falling rock."
(Joan moaned and hid her face in her hands.)
"It was useless to do anything so I left her there.
Why say anything when no one knew?
She was destroyed by the strike she had started.

The mines were shut down for good of course,
I couldn't bear the memory.
They would have had to be shut anyway,
we were losing money on them."
"And that's why Daddy never knew what happened to Mother,
raising me all by himself, and took to drink . . ."
"Yes, and I went back home to my wife and our little John was
           born
and I tried to forget . . ."
"Promise me one thing, Mr. Wainrich," Joan said,
"for the sake of my mother's memory,
that you'll open the mines again and give Daddy back his old job."

Joan had a lot to think about in the days that followed.
One day she got a call to come up right away to the big house,
and arriving, found John's wife dying,
having given birth to a child, and asking for her.
The pale bride lay holding her child, the Wainrich heir,
but seeing Joan, she sat up with her last strength and said,
"I give him to you," and fell back dead.
Joan fainted away, and when she came to,
it seemed a long time later, after the funeral and the mourning,
John Wainrich held her in his arms and was saying over and over,
"I am yours now, she gave me to you."
"But she meant the child," Joan cried.
"Both of us are yours, my darling."

So Joan found her place in life at last.
They always said she'd make it up there, surrounded by the help,
a lady, moving gracefully among the guests.
And what a difference now:
the miners in tuxes standing around the punchbowl with the
           swells,
the colored butler joining in the fun with loud yaks,
a new era, the classless society,
brought about by the smartest little woman in the U.S.A.,
Ladies and Gentlemen: Miss Joan Crawford.

NANCY

When scolded by Aunt Fritzy Ritz
Nancy seems to lose her wits.
Nancy is very often cross
but Fritzy's the undisputed boss.
She sits in the house reading the papers
supervising Nancy's capers.

Aunt Fritzy's a peculiar sort:
She has no visible means of support.
She never seems to earn a bean
and there's no "uncle" on the scene.
The questions seem to rise a lot:
is Fritzy Nancy's aunt or not?
If Fritzy is related to
that awful Mrs. Meany who
Annie Roonie had to flee,
then who can Nancy really be?

Rumors are flying thick and fast;
stories from mouth to ear are passed:
"Who is Fritzy Ritz indeed
but someone overcome by greed.
Welfare pays a monthly sum
to keep that orphan in her home.
Although she looks like Etta Kett
she'd older, more depraved, in debt."

One scandalous version I have heard
(of which I don't believe a word)
says Nancy's father, coming back
a little early from the track,
found his wife and Fritzy in
a most revolting act of sin.

With a knife he tried to nip
this lesbian relationship:
saw red, and stabbed; the blow went wild
and made an orphan of his child.
His wife was dead, he got the chair,
the court named Fritzy Ritz as heir.
The child, the house, the bank account,
were left to Fritzy Ritz, the "aunt."

No one will make Aunt Fritzy crawl
now that she's in charge of all:
the house, the grounds, the little brat.
She'll teach her to remember that!

Poor Nancy's nature has been bent
by this negative environment.
She never will grow up at all
but stay forever three feet tall.

THE TAILSPIN

Going into a tailspin
in those days meant curtains.
No matter how hard you pulled back on the stick
the nose of the plane wouldn't come up.

Spinning round, headed for a target of earth,
the whine of death in the wing struts,
instinct made you try to pull out of it that way, by force,
and for years aviators spiraled down and crashed.

Who could have dreamed that the solution
to this dreaded aeronautical problem
was so simple?
Every student flier learns this nowadays:
you move the joystick in the direction of the spin
and like a miracle the plane stops turning
and you are in control again
to pull the nose up out of the dive.

In panic we want to push the stick away from the spin,
wrestle the plane out of it,
but the trick is, as in everything,
to go with the turning willingly,
rather than fight, give in, go with it,
and that way come out of your tailspin whole.

BEAUTY CURE

from the Inuit

When I was just a girl
I once took a beauty treatment
recommended by our medicine man:
Grandma took me out
and found old dried-up dog turds for me.
I had to put each turd on my tongue
keeping it in my mouth until it was soft,
then rub myself with it
all over my breasts and stomach.
That is where I got my lovely figure and vitality from.
For as the medicine man said,
dogshit used in the right way
possesses magic powers
and is a kind of elixir of youth.
That is why I still look so young
in spite of my great age.
So for a beautiful complexion, ladies,
I do not hesitate to recommend dogshit lotion to you.
Try some today!

World War II

It was over Target Berlin the flak shot up our plane
just as we were dumping bombs on the already smoking city
on signal from the lead bomber in the squadron.
The plane jumped again and again as the shells burst under us
sending jagged pieces of steel rattling through our fuselage.
It was pure chance
that none of us got ripped by those fragments.

Then, being hit, we had to drop out of formation right away
losing speed and altitude,
and when I figured out our course with trembling hands on the
                instruments
(I was navigator)
we set out on the long trip home to England
alone, with two of our four engines gone
and gas streaming out of holes in the wing tanks.
That morning at briefing
we had been warned not to go to nearby Poland
partly liberated then by the Russians,
although later we learned that another crew in trouble
had landed there anyway,
and patching up their plane somehow,
returned gradually to England
roundabout by way of Turkey and North Africa.
But we chose England, and luckily
the Germans had no fighters to send up after us then
for this was just before they developed their jet.
To lighten our load we threw out
guns and ammunition, my navigation books, all the junk
and, in a long descent, made it over Holland
with a few goodbye fireworks from the shore guns.

Over the North Sea the third engine gave out
and we dropped low over the water.
The gas gauge read empty but by keeping the nose down
a little gas at the bottom of the tank sloshed forward
and kept our single engine going.
High overhead, the squadrons were flying home in formation
—the raids had gone on for hours after us.
Did they see us down there skimming the waves?
We radioed our final position for help to come
but had no idea if anyone
happened to be tuned in and heard us,
and we crouched together on the floor
knees drawn up and head down
in regulation position for ditching;
listened as the engine stopped, a terrible silence,
and we went down into the sea with a crash,
just like hitting a brick wall,
jarring bones, teeth, eyeballs panicky.
Who would ever think water could be so hard?
You black out, and then come to
with water rushing in like a sinking-ship movie.

All ten of us started getting out of there fast:
there was a convenient door in the roof to climb out by,
one at a time. We stood in line,
water up to our thighs and rising.
The plane was supposed to float for twenty seconds
but with all those flak holes
who could say how long it really would?
The two life rafts popped out of the sides into the water
but one of them only half-inflated
and the other couldn't hold everyone
although they all piled into it, except the pilot,
who got into the limp raft that just floated.
The radio operator and I, out last,
(did that mean we were least aggressive, least likely to survive?)
we stood on the wing watching the two rafts
being swept off by waves in different directions.
We had to swim for it.

Later they said the cords holding rafts to plane
broke by themselves, but I wouldn't have blamed them
for cutting them loose, for fear
that by waiting for us the plane would go down
and drag them with it.

I headed for the overcrowded good raft
and after a clumsy swim in soaked heavy flying clothes
got there and hung onto the side.
The radio operator went for the half-inflated raft
where the pilot lay with water sloshing over him,
but he couldn't swim, even with his life vest on,
being from the Great Plains—
his strong farmer's body didn't know
how to wallow through the water properly
and a wild current seemed to sweep him farther off.
One minute we saw him on top of a swell
and perhaps we glanced away for a minute
but when we looked again he was gone—
just as the plane went down sometime around then
when nobody was looking.

It was midwinter and the waves were mountains
and the water ice water.
You could live in it twenty-five minutes
the Ditching Survival Manual said.
Since most of the crew were squeezed on my raft
I had to stay in the water hanging on.
My raft? It was their raft, they got there first so they would live.
Twenty-five minutes I had.
Live, live, I said to myself.
You've got to live.
There looked like plenty of room on the raft
from where I was and I said so
but they said no.
When I figured the twenty-five minutes were about up
and I was getting numb,
I said I couldn't hold on anymore,
and a little rat-faced boy from Alabama, one of the gunners,

got into the icy water in my place,
and I got on the raft in his.
He insisted on taking off his flying clothes
which was probably his downfall because even wet clothes are
                    protection,
and then worked hard, kicking with his legs, and we all paddled,
to get to the other raft
and tie them together.
The gunner got in the raft with the pilot
and lay in the wet.
Shortly after, the pilot started gurgling green foam from his
                    mouth—
maybe he was injured in the crash against the instruments—
and by the time we were rescued,
he and the little gunner were both dead.

That boy who took my place in the water
who died instead of me
I don't remember his name even.
It was like those who survived the death camps
by letting others go into the ovens in their place.
It was him or me, and I made up my mind to live.
I'm a good swimmer,
but I didn't swim off in that scary sea
looking for the radio operator when he was washed away.
I suppose, then, once and for all,
I chose to live rather than be a hero, as I still do today,
although at that time I believed in being heroic, in saving the
                    world,
even if, when opportunity knocked,
I instinctively chose survival.

As evening fell the waves calmed down
and we spotted a boat, not far off, and signaled with a flare gun,
hoping it was English not German.
The only two who cried on being found
were me and a boy from Boston, a gunner.
The rest of the crew kept straight faces.

It was a British air-sea rescue boat:
they hoisted us up on deck,
dried off the living and gave us whisky and put us to bed,
and rolled the dead up in blankets,
and delivered us all to a hospital on shore
for treatment or disposal.
None of us even caught cold, only the dead.

This was a minor accident of war:
two weeks in a rest camp at Southport on the Irish Sea
and we were back at Grafton-Underwood, our base,
ready for combat again,
the dead crewmen replaced by living ones,
and went on hauling bombs over the continent of Europe,
destroying the Germans and their cities.

SWEET GWENDOLYN AND THE COUNTESS

The Countess rode out on her black horse in spring
wearing her black leather riding costume.
She was scouting for disciples in the countryside
and flicked with her whip the rosebuds as she passed.

Sweet Gwendolyn in her white dress
was out gathering May flowers.
Under sunshade hat, her pale face
blushed to the singing bees,
and her golden curls lay passive on bent shoulders
as she stooped to pluck a white lily.

The Countess passing by took one look,
galloped up, and reined her stallion sharply in,
high over the modest figure
of Sweet Gwendolyn with the downcast eyes.
She leaped down from her horse and knelt,
laying the whip in tribute before the golden girl.

That foolish one swooned forward to the ground
in a great white puff of dress fabric
and a scattering of flowers. At that,
the Countess rose in all her black pride
and put her dirty leather boot hard on Gwendolyn's bent neck,
pushing down the golden head to the grass,
and gave her a smart lash across her innocently upturned behind.

Gwendolyn looked up with begging eyes
and a small whimper of submission,
as the Countess pushed her over and threw the skirt up,
exposing legs and bottom bare,

and shoved the leather whip handle between squeezed thighs of
        virtue
forcing them apart to reveal the pink pulsing maidenhood.

Foolish Gwendolyn for not wearing panties
but how could she have known what was in store?
Her skirt fell over her head like petals of a fully-opened flower
and her legs waved in the air like stamen and pistil,
inviting the bee of the Countess's tongue
to slip in and sip nectar in the golden fuzz.

Poor Gwendolyn moaned with shame and pain
as she lay back crushing her May flowers, exposed and
        unresisting—
until the Countess, in full charge, pulled her to her feet,
tied the whip end around her neck,
remounted the big black horse
and slowly trotted off,
leading the sobbing girl a captive behind her
off to her dark castle.

Toothy Lurkers

The shores are patrolled by sharks,
east coast and west alike,
Don't look, they're there all right—

better squeeze shut your eyes
as you dunk yourself
in the sharky sea.

Right now my greatest fear
is to wake up and find myself
floating with bare toes.

How do surfers dare
go so far out
with those toothy lurkers in the waves?

BOTH MY GRANDMOTHERS

I. My Polish Grandma

Grandma and the children left at night.
It was forbidden to go. In those days
the Czar and his cossacks rode through the town at whim
killing Jews and setting fire to straw roofs
while just down the road the local Poles
sat laughing as they drank liquor.

Grandpa had gone to America first
and earned the money for the rest of the family to come over.
So they left finally, the whole brood of them
with the hired agent running the show,
an impatient man, and there were so many kids
and the bundles kept falling apart
and poor grandma was frightened of him.

She gave the man all the money
but she couldn't round up the kids fast enough for him.
They were children after all and didn't understand
and she was so stupid and clumsy herself,
carrying food for all of them and their clothes
and could she leave behind her pots?
Her legs hurt already; they were always swollen
from the hard work, the childbearing, and the cold.

They caught the train and there was a terrible moment
when the conductor came by for the tickets:
The children mustn't speak or he would know they were Jewish,
they had no permits to travel—Jews weren't allowed.
But the agent knew how to handle it,
everybody got *shmeared,* that means money got you everywhere.

The border was the worst. They had to sneak across at night.
The children mustn't make a sound, not even the babies.
Momma was six and she didn't want to do anything wrong
but she wasn't sure what to do.
The man led them through the woods
and beyond they could hear dogs barking from the sentry hut,
and then they had to run all of them down the ravine to the
             other side,
grandma broken down from childbearing with her bundles
and bad legs and a baby in her arms,
they ran all the children across the border
or the guards might shoot them
and if the little ones cried, the agent said he would smother them.

They got to a port finally.
Grandma had arranged for cabin passage, not steerage,
but the agent cheated and put them in the hold
so they were on the low deck looking up at the rich people.
My momma told me how grandma took care of all her children,
how Jake didn't move anymore he was so seasick, maybe even
             dead,
and if people thought he was dead
they would throw him overboard like garbage, so she hid him.
The rich tossed down oranges to the poor children—
my momma had never had one before.

They came to New York, to the tenements,
a fearful new place, a city, country people in the city.
My momma, who had been roly-poly in slow Poland,
got skinny and pimply in zippy New York.
Everybody grew up in a new way.
And now my grandma is dead and my momma is old
and we her children are all scattered over the earth
speaking a different language and forgetting
why it was so important
to go to a new country.

II. My Russian Grandma

When my father's father went to America
to earn the money for the family to come over later
my grandma had to take care of all six kids alone.

One day coming home from market,
with a baby in one arm and a bag of potatoes in the other,
she was crossing the tracks not paying attention
when she saw the train coming right up on her.
She jumped, dropping potatoes and baby on the tracks
as the train passed over
cutting the child to pieces; and in her grief
she reached under the turning wheels
to pick up the pieces of her baby
and got half her fingers cut off
and a bang on the head that knocked her cold.

Strangers took her to the hospital
where she came to, not knowing who she was or where she
         was—
it was a blessing for her to forget for a while.

But meanwhile the children were left alone.
When their mama didn't come
they huddled in the house afraid and crying,
except my father who went out to beg for food.
He kept them alive for all those terrible months.

And when grandma finally came home from the hospital
with her hands bandaged and anyway useless now
she found them all covered with lice and filthy,
and got to work like a whirlwind
to clean them up as best she could.
But it was too late: the hunger had weakened them
and the lice brought fever,
and they all died but my father and one girl.

Then with the house half-empty
and in her bitterness and sorrow
my grandma took a lover—who could blame her
for needing a man at such a time?
Perhaps at first he was just a boarder
she took in to help with expenses.
But my father who had taken charge of the family
hated him and tried to throw him out
the way little boys do, so the man beat him,
and my father took to cowering behind the furniture
living such a life of horror and fear
that he still stammers from it.

The money came from America eventually
and grandma and her two remaining children left Russia forever.
She would die in the new land of an earache,
my grandma who put sugar in my father's soup to fatten him
              up—
if he got fat she would know he was consoled.

My sister Barbara, being the first girl
born after grandma's death,
should have been named Marsha after her,
according to our traditions
of reincarnating the dead in the living
(as I should have been called Abraham
after my great-grandfather, now unknown to me forever).

Historians aren't writing our histories
so it is up to us to do it for ourselves,
but I know so little: this legend and her name.

Well, before everything is finally lost to us all
I write this remnant down.

GIANT PACIFIC OCTOPUS

I live with a giant pacific octopus:
he settles himself down beside me on the couch in the evening.
With two arms he holds a book
that he reads with his single eye:
he wears a pair of glasses over it for reading.

Two more arms go walking over to the sideboard across the room
where the crackers and cheese spread he loves are,
and they send back endless canapés, like a conveyor belt.

While his mouth is drooling and chomping,
another arm comes over and gropes me lightly:
it is like a breeze on my balls, that sweet tentacle.

Other arms start slipping around my body under my clothes.
They wiggle right in, one around my waist,
and all over, and down the crack of my ass.

I am drawn into his midst where his hot mouth waits for kisses
and I kiss him and make him into a boy
as all giant pacific octopuses are really
when you take them into your arms.

All their arms fluttering around you
become everywhere sensations of pleasure.
So, his sweet eye looks at me and his little mouth kisses me
and I swear he has the body of a greek god,
my giant pacific octopus boychik.

So this was what was in store
when I first saw him in the aquarium
huddled miserably on the rock

ignoring the feast of live crabs
they put in his windowed swimming pool.

You take home a creature like that, who needs love,
who is a mess when you meet
but who can open up like a flower with petal arms waving
                around — a beauty —
and it is a total pleasure to have him around,
even collapsible as he is like a big toy,
for as long as he will stay, one night or a lifetime,
for as long as god will let you have him.

from Eskimo Songs and Stories (1973)

THE GIANT BEAR
from the Inuit

There once was a giant bear
who followed people for his prey.
He was so big he swallowed them whole:
then they smothered to death inside him
if they hadn't already died of fright.

Either the bear attacked them on the run,
or if they crawled into a cave
where he could not squeeze his body in,
he stabbed them with his whiskers like toothpicks,
drawing them out one by one,
and gulped them down.

No one knew what to do
until a wise man went out and let the bear swallow him,
sliding right down his throat into the dark, hot, slimy stomach.
And once inside, took his knife
and simply cut him open,
killing him of course.

He carved a door in the bear's belly
and threw out those who had been eaten before,
and then out he stepped himself
and went home to get help with the butchering.

Everyone lived on bear meat for a long time.
That's the way it goes:
monster one minute, food the next.

GRANDMA TAKES A FOSTER CHILD
from the Inuit

Grandma turned a little odd in spring:
she took a caterpillar in and mothered it.
She put it down her sleeve
while she went about her work,
letting it suck like a baby on her skin,
and soon it grew so big and fat and happy
it said, Jeetsee-jeetsee.

Her grandchildren saw this and were disgusted—
after all, a caterpillar!
So when Grandma went behind the tent to pee,
they threw it to the sled-dogs
who gobbled the juicy tidbit up.

And when Grandma came back in
she called, My darling? My own one?
Why don't I hear the song that made my old heart young again?
Where is my dear one that went Jeetsee?
Gone?
And she sat down crying by the fire alone.

THE WOMAN WHO TURNED TO STONE
from the Inuit

A woman once refused to get married
and turned down every man who proposed to her,
so finally one of them said:
"You've got a heart of stone
I hope you turn into stone!"
And before she could answer with her famous sharp tongue
his words began to come true
and she could no longer move
from the spot where she was standing by the lake.
She was really turning into stone from the legs up.
Desperately she called to some kayaks paddling by:
"Kayaks, please come here boys,
I'm ready to get married now."
(Now she was willing to marry not just one
but as many as she could get!)
But the men wouldn't come near her
having been rejected too often.
She clapped her hands and sang her song:
"Kayaks everywhere,
please come here,
I'll take you all as husbands now.
Men, have pity on me
before my precious hands
have turned to stone."
But then her hands turned to stone,
stone was her tongue,
and her song was done.

LAZY ESKIMO
from the Inuit

When I go out for caribou cow
I get myself a caribou cow.
But my friend, some hunter he is:
he's lazy as a dog. Big shot,
he's lying in the igloo dreaming of big game.

Friend, you'd better practice on caribou
before you go out on the ice
and face the claws and jaws of the white bear
or the horns of the musk ox charging you,
poor you and your little spear.

from STARS IN MY EYES (1978)

MAE WEST

She comes on drenched in a perfume called Self-Satisfaction
from feather boa to silver pumps.

She does not need to be loved by you
though she'll give you credit for good taste.
Just because you say you love her
she's not throwing herself at your feet in gratitude.

Every other star reveals how worthless she feels
by crying when the hero says he loves her,
or how unhoped-for the approval is
when the audience applauds her big number—
but Mae West takes it as her due:
she knows she's good.

She expects the best for herself
and knows she's worth what she costs
and she costs plenty—
she's not giving anything away.

She enjoys her admirers, fat daddy or muscleman,
and doesn't confuse vanity and sex,
though she never turns down pleasure,
lapping it up.

Above all she enjoys her self,
swinging her body that says, Me, me, me, me,
Why not have a good time?
As long as you amuse me, go on,
I like you slobbering over my hand, big boy—
I have a right to.

Most convincing, we know all this
not by her preaching
but by her presence—it's no act.
Every word and look and movement
spells Independence:
she likes being herself.

And we who don't
can only look on, astonished.

An island in the fog. Waves lapping.
Strange movements. Figures digging graves.
Our boat approaches silently.
We have come to rescue Divina
from the mad doctor
who uses the blood of virgins
for a serum to restore his wife's beauty,
poor Madame Imperia who always wears a mask
imploring him to work harder, cursing her fate.

He has an army of half-human slaves,
their brains replaced by those of dogs,
and a chief assistant Igor,
whose mother was a Siberian witch
and his father a British scientist on an expedition
to locate frozen mammoths
for a meat-packing concern.
Igor rules the army of dogmen
with a whip and a sharp boot in the butt.

Now as we come nearer there is the sound
of barking voices, shovels on stone,
and an occasional yelping
as Igor kicks a lazy cur in the ribs
or the whip separates snarling mad dogmen
going for each others' throats.

Are we too late?
Have they already drained Divina's blood
for the vain Madame Imperia
to make her young again?
The boat slips into the cove,
we gather up the equipment for the rescue

253

and steal into the woods around the house
of mad doctor Cranshaw,
a benevolent-looking dwarf from Groton, Massachusetts,
who fell into the clutches of Madame Imperia.
She had chosen him
because of his high marks in chemistry at M.I.T.
and his personal fortune
for she knew that getting back your looks costs plenty.
They were married at a society wedding in Newport
after which she took off her undetectable plastic face
and showed him her true one, so horrible
that he bought the island and set up a laboratory there
to search for a lotion
that would restore her beauty.

Now for twenty years girls had been disappearing
until most recently our heroine Divina
was snatched from her prayers
at the grotto of Our Lady of Loreto.
At first everyone supposed she had run off to be a hippy.
That's where girls used to go,
into the international druggy scene
until they turned up in a basement dead
from the O.D.'s with tracks up and down their arms,
or sometimes with two little teeth marks at the throat
and strangely drained of blood.
Divina had dropped acid a few times
but she was no junkie,
and she was into the I Ching and the Jesus prayer
but she was no hippy.
Anyway, nobody is a hippy anymore.
Nowadays girls go into the feminist movement,
and if they disappear, it's into the radical lesbian underground
holding up banks and blowing up bridges.
Well, Divina had swung a little both ways —
we both led a hip life-style —
but she was no dyke, I'll swear to that.
She was really crazy about me, if you know what I mean —
she was my chick, she was in trouble,

so the Chief assigned me to the case:
It was ready Eddie to the rescue!

Now we were approaching the house through the dark trees,
brushing away cobwebs from our faces, ugh.
In a clearing ahead two dogmen carried something
horrible and writhing off into the bushes.
Inside the house through the lighted windows
the doctor was experimenting on one of the dogmen.
Everybody was busy at his tasks
except Madame Imperia
who only sat around veiled and cursing,
ordering the dogmen to bring her this and that,
polishing her nails, and filing them razor sharp.

Forward. We plant a stick
of nerve gas by the window
and set it off with a glass-shattering boom.
All inhabitants are paralyzed for fifteen minutes.
We race through the house calling Divina. Divina.
No Divina.
The mad dwarf doctor's eyes are bulging
and Madame Imperia's are glittering,
and Igor has murder in his—
for the gas does not put you out
and your brain goes right on figuring
and they were all thinking what to do about us
when the gas wore off:
They had a few tricks up their sleeves all right.

Minutes were ticking by. Ah, cages.
But we don't dare let loose the sub-human monsters there,
all operated on unsuccessfully by the mad Cranshaw.
Now a door to the basement, but sealed.
Search for a button in the wall.
No, not a button, an electric eye.
Break the beam and the door slides open.
Steps going down, an underground lab
with who? Yes, Divina

strapped to a table
breasts bulging up from thongs cutting into her flesh,
thighs writhing to protect her tender loins.
From the look of things
those dogmen had been having quite a go at her,
but apart from slaver on her face
and puddles of green dog come on her belly
it doesn't look like it has done her any harm
although she'll probably need a few weekends at Esalen
to straighten out her head.

Divina darling, I've come to free you.
But Divina's eyes are like stoned.
Has she been given a dog's brain already?

Oy, the fifteen minutes are up
and the whole pack of loonies burst in, grab us,
tie us up, and proceed with the operation.
There must be something to do, but it seems hopeless.

While the faithful Igor prepared the surgical instruments
and swung the great radiotrope into place
that directed the plastrons to the surgery,
the dwarf doctor took a great book off a bible-stand
and held it before us, turning the pages,
his eyes misty with memory:
"Here is my Book of the Dead," he said,
"the record of my experiments, my life work.
In the early stages I had such childish ideas,
that the serum could be made from blood and hair,
from flesh even." He riffled through
page after page of virgin sacrificed.
"But now I know it is a vibration one must catch.
I have the secret at last and tonight
I will finish my work: We will have the serum."
Madame Imperia could not resist giving a triumphant shriek.
"You mean," I said, "there will be no sacrifice of life?"
"No, she shall be alive and well . . . well, almost. . . ."
Here the mad dwarf faltered.

We strained at the bonds desperately. "What do you mean?"
"She will lack her . . . ah . . . her organ of generation."
"You mean you are taking out her cunt, you creep?" we blurted.
"A trifle. She'll be otherwise perfect.
My wife will be beautiful again after a few well-placed injections,
and I'll be free to go back to my original interest,
the study of the generative cycle of the four-toed wallaby."
The monster! Now I was really mad.
With my tongue I pried off the false cap of my right molar
putting into action a radio transmitter.
By clicking teeth in Morse code
messages could be sent.
"Isle of Dead mission calling Headquarters," I clicked.
I must have looked like I had a severe case of the chatters.
"Send choppers in at once."
Meanwhile the doctor continued with his work
zeroing the radiotrope right into target.
There was no time to wait for helicopters, troops, Medicaid —
I had to act.
There was an emergency capsule in one of my left molars —
I broke it out and swallowed.
It contained a special drug
to give five minutes of superhuman strength
but it had to be used with caution
because immediately after that you passed out.
I had to take care of this situation in five minutes — or else.
The drug coursed through my veins, my chest swelled,
I felt like superman to the rescue.
I snapped my bonds easily,
took Igor by the throat with one hand,
and Dr. Cranshaw with the other,
and tied them like a big sandwich
with Madame Imperia in between clawing at them both,
as the pack of dogmen ran howling into the woods.
Of course I pulled the plug on the equipment at once.
And there was my Divina lying on the operating table,
her breasts bulging up at me, her eyes and wet lips
imploring me to come to her,
and with the superman drug in my veins

I had supersex to give her:
I felt it throbbing up in my loins.
That would bring her to her senses again if anything would.
When she saw the size of it she screamed,
then her brain clicked off, her eyes glazed,
and she started panting.
Give it to me, she moaned,
and ground her hips up as far as the thongs allowed her.
It's all for you baby, I said, and reached out
but she seemed to be getting further away from me.
I took bigger steps, but got slower and slower,
the earth whirled
and I slipped off into darkness.

When I awoke I was back at the stationhouse
on a couch in the locker room
and the Chief was leaning over me giving me a hand job saying,
Boy, you really need it bad.
I groaned and pushed him away.
Did you get Cranshaw and the others?

They're all behind bars
and we've got the dogcatcher rounding up the dogmen.
We hope to place them in good homes.
Divina has already made an application for a couple of them.

Where's Divina, Boss? Were we too late?

She'll be better than ever, Sonny,
once her cunt cools off.
The doc is putting ice cubes up it.

And Madame Imperia?

She completely flipped out I'm afraid,
but you know, it's a mystery to me
because in the struggle to get a hold of her
her mask ripped off

and there was nothing wrong with her.
In fact, she was a darn good-looking dame.

Then the doctor must have discovered the serum
but they were too crazy already
to know they had succeeded.
That book of his must be worth a fortune.

You mean the book he was raving about,
his Book of the Dead?

Yes, get it and put it under lock and key.
We're going to be on easy street.

Oh shit, Sonny, I guess I didn't tell you.
There was a little fire—or rather a big one—
and the whole joint burned down—
you know those old houses.

Then our only hope is the doctor.
He'll know the secret.

The doctor? He's completely nuts.

Then I'd advise giving him a little laboratory to play around in
in the nuthouse, and a free hand
to experiment on the inmates
and a big book to write in.
I'll bet Revlon will finance the whole thing.

Just as the Chief turned back to his dirty picture book
with his hand stealing fondly into his open fly
the phone rang and he picked it up:
"What the hell you say? A thing? What kind of thing?
You say this thing came out of a lab at Caltech
when the chemicals were all spilled during the earthquake
and has been what? Eating co-eds
and getting bigger and bigger?
I thought it was a boys' school?

Oh, Women's Lib had a demonstration there and things
        changed. . . .
I'll send my man right over to investigate.
Yeah, he's the one who cracked the Cranshaw case."

So there went my vacation. I was on a new case,
one that would prove to be the toughest in my career,
fighting an extra-terrestrial blob
that made people into zombies . . .
but that's another story.

from A FULL HEART (1977)

NEW YORK

I live in a beautiful place, a city
people claim to be astonished
when you say you live there.
They talk of junkies, muggings, dirt, and noise,
missing the point completely.

I tell them where they live it is hell,
a land of frozen people.
They never think of people.

Home, I am astonished by this environment
that is also a form of nature
like those paradises of trees and grass

but this is a people paradise
where we are the creatures mostly,
though thank God for dogs, cats, sparrows, and roaches.

This vertical place is no more an accident
than the Himalayas are.
The city needs all those tall buildings
to contain the tremendous energy here.
The landscape is in a state of balance.
We do God's will whether we know it or not:
where I live the streets end in a river of sunlight.

Nowhere else in the country do people
show just what they feel—
we don't put on any act.
Look at the way New Yorkers
walk down the street. It says,
I don't care. What nerve,

to dare to live their dreams, or nightmares,
and no one bothers to look.

True, you have to be an expert to live here.
Part of the trick is not to go anywhere, lounge about,
go slowly in the midst of the rush for novelty.
Anyway, besides the eats the big event here
is the streets, which are full of love —
we hug and kiss a lot. You can't say that
for anywhere else around. For some
it's a carnival of sex —
there's all the opportunity in the world.
For me it is no different:
out walking, my soul seeks its food.
It knows what it wants.
Instantly it recognizes its mate, our eyes meet,
and our beings exchange a vital energy,
the universe goes on Charge
and we pass by without holding.

ROACHES

An old decrepit city like London
doesn't have any.
They ought to love it there
in those smelly, elegant buildings.
Surely I myself have smuggled some in in my luggage
but they obviously don't like the English—
for that alone I should love them.

They are among the brightest
and most attractive of small creatures
though you have to be prepared
for the look of horror
on the faces of out-of-town guests
when a large roach walks across the floor
as you are sipping drinks.
You reach out and swat,
and keeping the conversation going
pick up the corpse and drop it into an ashtray
feeling very New Yorky doing it.
After all, you've got to be tough to live here—
the visitor didn't make it.

Roaches also thrive on it here:
they set up lively communes
in open boxes of rice, spaghetti, and matzohs.
You come in to make coffee in the morning
and find a dead one floating in the kettle
and dots of roach shit on the dishes,
hinting at roachy revels the night before.

If you let them alone
they stop running at the sight of you
and whisker about

taking a certain interest in whatever you are doing,
and the little ones, expecting like all babies to be adored,
frolic innocently in the sink,
even in daytime when grownup roaches rest
after a night of swarming around the garbage bag.
The trouble with this approach is
they outbreed you and take over,
even moving sociably right into your bed.

Which brings up the question, Do they bite?
Some say yes, and if yes,
do they carry Oriental diseases?
Even though you have tried to accept them
there comes a point when you find your eyes
studying labels of roach killers on supermarket shelves,
decide to try a minimal approach, buy one,
but when you attack with spray can aimed
they quickly learn to flee.
The fastest of course live to multiply
so they get cleverer all the time
with kamikaze leaping into space,
or zigzagging away,
race into far corners of the apartment
where they drop egg-sacs in their last throes
to start ineradicable new colonies.

When you light the oven
they come out and dance on the hot stove top
clinging with the tips of their toes,
surviving by quick footwork until you swat them.
Or if you spray it first
you have the smell of roaches roasting slowly.

And when you wash them down the drain
without their being certifiably dead
do they crawl up when the coast is clear?
Some even survive the deadliest poisons devised by man
and you have weird, white mutations running about.
Dying, they climb the walls, or up your legs in agony,

making you feel like a dirty rat,
until they fall upside down with frail legs
waving in the air.

No more half-measures—
it's them or us you finally realize
and decide on nothing less than total fumigation:
the man comes while you are out
and you return to a silent apartment, blissfully roach-free.
You vacuum up the scattered bodies of the unlucky,
pushing down guilty feelings, lonely feelings,
and congratulate yourself.

                        You booby,
they have only moved over to the neighbor's
who is now also forced to fumigate,
and just when you are on the princess phone crowing to your
               friends,
back they come, the whole tribe of them,
many gone now
due to their trivial life span and chemical adversaries
but more numerous than ever with the newborn
and all the relatives from next door and the neighborhood with
               them,
you standing there outraged, but secretly relieved
as they swarm into the kitchen from every crevice,
glad to be home, the eternal innocents,
greeting you joyfully.

AFTER THE MOONWALK

When they landed on the moon
what we really wanted
was for strange creatures to seize them.

We wanted them to take off their helmets
and discover they could breathe,
that science was wrong
and there was air there.

We wanted people to be there,
tiny people who got that way
because they failed to develop usefully
and finally were banished
into a universe of rejected experiments.
And insects, perhaps the giant ancestors
of our own ants and bees.

When they took the first step on the moon
we wanted green insect men with mandibles and pincers
to rush out and right on television
drag them off to glass-enclosed cities,
or to underground factories and mines
where a humanoid race toils
that once ruled the moon
but invented nuclear weapons and destroyed it
and are now the slaves of giant ants who took over—
all this revealed before our eyes—
and an appeal for funds
to build a fleet of airships to attack the moon
and rescue our astronauts in captivity.

Instead what happened
was more like the way we once came to this continent

seeing nothing of value in the people here,
like an invading cancer cell
(though perhaps even the cancerous cell obeys laws
that are still beyond our understanding).

Our earth-probe succeeded
in breaking through the moon's defenses,
destroying forever what it was
but opening a path for settlers.
What we left on the moon, the first gift of mankind,
was a pile of garbage.

And if it isn't yet a living world in our sense
(though what in the universe is dead? It's all alive)
we have sent our germ cells
to start multiplying there:
even now air seeds may be growing
an atmosphere like ours.

And when it is ready to be on its own
to search for its own orbit,
what great wrenching away is ahead
and dislocations of the stars,
tidal waves and firestorms on earth,
repeating the destruction of continents
when the moon was born like a baby from our oceans.

What was begun—and it began long ago,
the necessity for a moon—
must continue to the end,
with us sitting as long as we can,
glued to our TV sets,
watching it all.

THE RESERVOIR

The ancient reservoir,
an underground lake beneath the city,
has been closed to the public by the government
due to stringent budget cuts.

The news fills me with dismay.
It was the only thing I cared about
in that city of minarets, domes, and ruined palaces.
And to think I could have seen it
but passed it by, dismissing it
as a minor tourist attraction, not worth
spending fifteen minutes or fifty cents on.

I suppose there was nothing much to it:
you could go out on it in a boat,
though it has never been fully explored.
But imagine a city having a source of sweet water under it,
not needing aqueducts or to use the polluted river.

And maybe even it was a city underground,
now flooded, as the sewers of modern Jerusalem
once were Roman streets.

Too late I realize it was one of the important things.

It was closed for centuries
before being rediscovered and opened again.
And even if the population
never thought or even knew about it
still its presence must have affected them.
Like a desert is an energy accumulator,
a mountain a magnetic pole,
bodies of water give off an exciting influence.

Now it is shut again
and those carved pillars of limestone
that stretch away into the gloom
may collapse and the whole thing fill up with garbage,
become a sewer instead of a reservoir,
that underground lake, sacred to dervishes,
lost track of, and profaned.

And for how long, O my people,
I cry from the bottom of my wretched heart,
will it still be possible to reopen it, and explore?

A Full Heart

My mother's family was made up of loving women.
They were, on the whole, bearers,
though Esther, the rich sister, had only one,
she was the exception.

Sarah, the oldest, had five with her first husband
(that was still in Poland),
was widowed and came here
where she married a man with four of his own,
and together they had another five,
all of whom she raised, feeding them in relays,
except little Tillie who sat in the kitchen
and ate with everyone, meaning all the time,
resulting in a fat figure
that made her despair of ever finding a husband,
but miraculously she did,
for God has decreed there is someone for everyone,
if you're desperate enough
and will take what you can get.

Aunt Rachel had twelve, raising them in a stable.
She was married to a junk dealer
who kept horses to haul the wagons.
He was famous for his stinginess
so they lived in a shack surrounded by bales of hay.
That was in America, in a slum called Bronzeville
that the black people have now inherited from the Jews,
God help them.
Then, as now, plenty of kids turned out bad,
going to work for that Jewish firm, Murder Incorporated,
or becoming junkies like one of my cousins did.

My mother had only six
but that's not counting . . . I'll say no more
than she was always pregnant,
with a fatalistic "What can you do?"
("Plenty," her friend Blanche replied—she was liberated.
"You don't have to breed like a rabbit.")
Like her mother who had a baby a year in Poland
until Grandpa left for America
giving her a rest.
There were women who kept bearing
even then, mysteriously, as from habit.

Women were always tired in those days and no wonder,
with the broken-down bodies they had
and their guts collapsed,
for with every child they got a dragging down.
My mother finally had hers
tied back up in the hospital and at the same time
they tied those over-fertile tubes,
which freed her from "God's terrible curse on women."

And not just the bearing, but the work:
The pots couldn't be big enough for those hungry broods—
Sarah used hospitals pots for hers.
And then the problem of filling the pots,
getting up at dawn to go to the fishing boats
for huge fish carcasses cheap,
buying bushels of half-spoiled vegetables for pennies,
begging the butcher for bones,
and then lugging it all home on their bad legs.
They didn't think of their looks for a minute,
and better they didn't, shapeless as life made them.
(And yet they remained attractive to their men,
by the evidence of their repeated pregnancies.)
They just went around wrecks, always depressed,
unable to cope, or hiding in bed
while the children screamed.
"Escape, escape, there must be escape"
was my mother's theme song, until at last

her children escaped from her and her misery,
having wrecked her life, that endless sacrifice,
for what?

I see the proletarian women like them on the streets,
cows with udders to the waist
lugging black oilcloth shopping bags,
the mamales, the mamacitas, the mammies,
the breeders of the world with loving eyes.
They sit around the kitchen table with full hearts
telling each other their troubles—
never enough money, the beasts their men are to them,
the sorrow life is for a woman, a mother,
the children turning out no good—
and feed each other pieces of leftover meat from the icebox
to make up a little for life's pain
and sighing, drink tea
and eat good bread and butter.

THE FAREWELL

They say the ice will hold
so there I go,
forced to believe them by my act of trusting people,
stepping out on it,

and naturally it gaps open
and I, forced to carry on coolly
by my act of being imperturbable,
slide erectly into the water wearing my captain's helmet,
waving to the shore with a sad smile,
"Goodbye my darlings, goodbye dear one,"
as the ice meets again over my head with a click.

THE LOST, DANCING
after Cavafy

When the drums come to your door
do not try to shut them out,
do not turn away and resist them,
for they have come to tell you what you need to hear,
they are your fate.
When Antony heard them
he knew then that he had lost Egypt forever.
He did not shriek or tear his clothes
for he always knew they would come someday.
What the drums speak to you
is so inevitable you have to agree with them—
nothing else could be right.
So when the drummers and dancers come to your door
your life changes,
and with no bitterness
but with a sad smile
—after all what you had you had,
you loved the way few men love—
and as someone who was worthy of such a kingdom,
join the army of the lost, dancing,
follow the drums
and turn and wave goodbye
to the Alexandria you are losing.

Rio de Janeiro
Carnival, 1974

The Sand Map

I am looking for the places
  that were there before the sand.

What is strange about this country,
  sphinxes and pyramids on a duny plain,
    is what emerges from the hidden.

Once they looked ordinary in their real setting,
  not desert, but a green,
    a populated world,

and now covered by sand
  its peaks are hints
    we try to make sense of,
      imagining we long for it.

We long for something all right
  and dream of finding a sand map to lead us there
    hoping that under the desert is where it is.

If not that, what are we longing for?
  What lost world? But what if
    it is for something new, not old,
      the not-yet-born?

And even with a sand map, an accurate one,
  say you follow it, trustingly,
    and discover that buried world
      with its glories, and horrors,

then what do you have?
  Even knowing what was there,

following a program of limited excavation
   won't bring it back,

won't make sands that cover it blow away,
   make those figures on friezes come to life,
   and the cataclysmic scenes replay.

For after you have found it,
   after all that searching and working,
      you'll have to look at your life and see
      that nothing has changed—

so, having dealt with the past as best you could
   you might declare it is better
   to know than not to know,

but having used up the best of your strength,
   weary now, you must live with what you are,
      and even if it is desert, where you are,
      making the best of it.

DAVID'S DREAM

*"You're not ready for
the convent yet."—D.D.T.*

He said that he dreamed
that everyone was meeting at the baths tonight
except me.
I'll be teaching there in the morning
so I couldn't go.

Well, he's got my number all right, I'm no fun.
I talk liberation
but my actions show otherwise,
and he dreams me as I really am,
a ruler-snapping nun
keeping the class in line.

My image is definitely bad.

I only show up at the baths
when morning guilt lights up the shabby linoleum
and the employees are scrubbing the love juice
off the walls and ceilings of the orgy room,
and the customers are putting on their jeans
anxious to go home.

That's when I arrive with my attendance book
and a sad sack stuffed with experience,
teaching what I don't believe in
and nobody wants to hear.

THE LESSON: If all you can do is teach
                        don't do it at the baths.
                  If you go to the baths
                        don't go in the morning.
                  And if you go into the steam room
                        Take off your habit, baby,
                        and leave your ruler home.

VISITING HOME

I.

It is an exercise in independence
not being like them.

Seeing that our bodies
are of the same nature
I religiously do my yoga
and stay open to other possibilities.

I remind myself I am allowed to shit.
So far I've been able to
though this morning I doubted.

Genital feelings nevertheless
are a long ways off.
They still have me by the balls.

My father and I suffer the same ailments:
electric leg in the night, back trouble,
prima donna stomach,
a ringing in the left ear.

My mother declares her goal
is not to have to do anything
(that's me too)
and she refuses to make any effort
even to save her life.

We suggest activities
but all she wants is to go away on a Greyhound bus,
live in hotels
and hang out in the lobby and cocktail lounge

280

talking to people.
Old ladies ought to be allowed.

I too am a roamer,
a talker with strangers,
but I have stars for travel
and she's stuck at home.

The trouble is she's one of the poor.
My father holds the purse strings
and it's as if he were still doling out to her
the daily allowance of five dollars
to feed the family on.
She will always believe in revolution
and be a feminist through and through.

By studying them
can I really know anything about myself?
But I can't stop.
Oh, all this concentrating for years
on what happened in childhood
to make me a mess,
all the analysis of transferences and dreams
to see how I repeat the defeat. . . .
All that rebellion against being like them.

II.

At lunch my father sits
hunched over his food
like some incredibly primitive
prehistoric man.

His face I feel as an unused
structure within my own. It is made
for glaring, raging, judging, criticizing.
I wish I could melt it down softer.

Under my mild looks
I have his skull, his features,
even his expression,
afraid of life, afraid of the flow.

We share an essential joylessness.
As I get older, that is starting to show
and it is a measure of our difficulties
that I will hate looking like him.

At the table he will hardly meet my eyes.
His slide away, masking a confusion of feelings.
Yet when I say I am going to leave
he gets a stricken look.

My mother shyly kisses me
half on the lips. It is sweet.
I think of my grandmother's huge soft wet kisses,
messages from another world of feeling
where nothing is held back.

My mother's eyes are wide open.
We gaze at each other and love flows.
My father and I can't seem to find a way
to let that happen.

What if I said to him, Daddy—
though it would be better in Yiddish,
the language he can express himself in—
Daddy, I don't want to go on for the rest of my life
with this barrier between us.

I don't blame you for the past,
my hellish childhood, and the years after,
that nightmare, when I didn't know how to live my life.
Let's try to be straight with each other,
though there is no ignoring the wreckage between us.

But it is as if I were waiting for him to start,
as though he alone had the key to that door
to what feels like the possibility of . . . of what?
a better life? a rootedness?
Making a vital connection it is hard to live without
to be whole.

III.

Before I was born he took the first step
in our estrangement
by changing his name from Feldman to Field
although even Feldman wasn't his name
(though he made Field mine).
In Europe it was Felscher
but at Immigration they wrote down Feldman.
And what's the difference,
wasn't that a good Jewish name?

As we came, he named us like lords and ladies:
Adele, Alice, Edward, Richard, Robert, and Barbara,
and moved as far from the Lower East Side as he could
to a town in the Anglo-Saxon Protestant world,
the real America.
He did not have to cope much with that,
as we did every day.
He went to work in the city
where, with his new name,
he was able to go into advertising,
at that time practically closed to Jews.
He couldn't talk to those people, or us
without stammering, or yelling.

He did not want to know
we hated the house, the block, the village
where the people didn't want us—
after all, that was his achievement in life.

The family was his world and he wanted it to be ours
and not adopt the alien ways around us.

He avoided the relatives from the old country—
even our grandparents we hardly knew.
He felt superior to them all.
We ate on Yom Kippur, though he didn't,
having a stomachache every year,
and mixed milk with meat,
though he drew the line at Christmas trees.

It wasn't even that he was trying not to be Jewish
but it was his way of being modern.
He and my mother spoke Yiddish together
but we never learned more
than the words for "don't hit him" or "to bed."
We were left out of the secret world
of their real identity.

When we asked about our religion
he said we were atheists, and we shocked everybody
by going around insisting on it.
But when we asked him our nationality
he said we were American Jews
which in our town just meant Jews.
And what does God have to do with it?
You don't need God to be a Jew.
Anyway, we were beaten up
whether we believed in God or not
for a Jew was automatically an atheist to them.
Or maybe we were beaten up
because everyone knew in those days before Israel
it was our role in life to be.

Some people once met in our house
discussing whether to convert for the sake of the children
to save us from the Nazis,
for surely what was happening in Germany
was possible where we lived

with the Bund meeting in the high schools
and swastikas painted all over—
but we knew nothing could be done
to make you anything but a Jew.
Change your name to Field
and they call you Fieldinsky.

There was a kind of native fascism there
where the people disliked everything darker,
everything foreign, races that bred fast,
with daughters developing large breasts early,
races that did not understand conformity
but stuck to what they were.

Everything closer to New York was inferior,
even girls living the next town nearer.
Speaking a foreign language was unthinkable
and having foreign parents unbearable.

They didn't like me and with good reason:
my long, hooked nose; kinky, black hair;
wrinkly skin on the back of my hands—
I was a small, skinny, dark, and dirty boy,
my prick was button-sized and circumcised,
my parents spoke Yiddish
and I had lots of sisters and brothers.
We were animals.

My father ignored everything.
He didn't want us to be like the townsfolk
but to be an enclave, a ghetto, with him the master.
He made rules. Many things were forbidden:
    to believe in God, heaven, angels, or ghosts—
        all superstitions;
    to listen to jazz or popular music—for the goyim—
        or chamber music, or Wagner or Sibelius—Nazis;
    to participate in school activities or sports—
        for the goyim who were not serious about life;

to care about your looks, clothes—
    tinsel, for the goyim;
to mind being different and want to be popular—
    contemptible;
and any evidence of sexuality was most forbidden—
    —for bums.
In short, it was forbidden to have fun.
Duties around the house came first,
practicing music, and homework.

My parents made fun of everyone,
the neighbor who claimed to like opera,
the girl who wanted to be a movie star;
this one spent cultural evenings,
that one fell for the flattery of salesgirls and men;
above all anyone who was pleased with himself
or spent money on his pleasures;
and of course the goyim for their narrow, orderly lives.
All the relatives were torn to bits.

There's the main sin of Jewish parents,
being overcritical,
so you grow up ashamed of yourself, worthless
(if they don't love you you must be worthless),
more critical of yourself than anyone could ever be,
ridiculing what you long for, what you need to go on living,
ashamed to admit you want love, or anything,
and denying it to the end.
Even ashamed of being ashamed.

You dream only of running away.
My soul, but not my lips, cried out,
"Doesn't anyone want a little boy?"
But there was nobody out there
who would ever want someone like me,
who would ever take me in.

My father's theory of child-raising
was that it doesn't matter what you do to them, what they hear—

you feed them, clothe them, house them, and train them,
and they grow up adults,
that state of being grownup I could hardly wait for,
and by some magic all the terror and guilt
and self-loathing would go away.
Our sexuality would start to function
the way it was expected to,
and we would become famous.
Or more important,
we wouldn't do anything to shame him.

IV.

Yiskidor, when he dies I won't know the Hebrew words to say.
Yiskidor, I won't be able to help the soul he doesn't believe in
        find rest.
Yiskidor, I go through life cut off from my ancestors.
Yiskidor, I live a life of shit.
Yiskidor, I'm a bum, I'm no man, I'm not even at the beginning.
Yiskidor, I don't know the prayers.
Yiskidor, I don't know the sacred rites.
Yiskidor, I buried my friend Alfred and it was done badly,
        nobody wailed, nobody tore their clothes—
        I didn't know you were supposed to,
        though somehow I felt like doing it.
Yiskidor, I took a clod of earth from the grave
        and have placed it in my shrine with his books
        and the letter from Jerusalem telling how he died
        of alcohol and drugs like a movie star,
        his dogs barking to alert the neighbors.
        He always reminded me of Marilyn Monroe—
        he had that ultimate glamour
        and went around in a cloud of admiration,
        though he never felt loved.
        Like a good Jew, he went to Jerusalem to die
        but his family brought him back
        and buried him in Staten Island.

Yiskidor, when the clods hit the coffin I bawled
and everybody turned and stared at me.

Yiskidor, I pray for my mother every way I can
though I don't know the prayers to protect her.
Yiskidor, how she suffers, my mommeh.
I promised I would take her to California when I
grew up
and we'd live in a house overlooking the ocean,
just so she wouldn't suffer anymore.
Yiskidor, what is my sacred duty to my parents
but to honor them, both in life and death,
for they produced me by the holy process,
Yiskidor, and if they fucked me up
they did not know what they were doing.

Yiskidor, and look what they gave me, the gifts,
my life's full of gifts, all my loves.
Yiskidor, for that little boy who didn't know it but was lucky,
with parents that made life hard,
Yiskidor, who complicated things for me
so I could never take the easy path
but had to choose my own
when all I wanted was to be standard:
straight hair, straight nose, straight.
Yiskidor, for that desperate wish I went to sleep with every night,
"When I wake up I'll look right, be popular,
They'll like me."

Yiskidor, I woke up at last and they liked me
(even if I don't like myself)
so I don't read the "How to be Popular" books anymore.
Now I read the "How to be Saved" books.
They all say, Awaken,
follow the path of the heart
which leads to the east.
There is no one to blame anymore
and what you become is up to you.

Yiskidor, and I believe them, I can't help it.
My family screams at me, Be skeptical.
I'd like to be but I can't.
Yiskidor, I see I had the perfect parents
for everything has turned out right
like a miracle.

Yiskidor, I had the illusion I could invent my Self,
I thought I could live by the rules of psychiatrists,
Yiskidor, I had the illusion I could get free of history,
not only our history, but my own history.
Yiskidor, but now I must go back to the beginning
if I can find it. It is surely somewhere
inside myself, still trapped
in that defeat at the first breath
when I understood my predicament—
when I chose.

Yiskidor, they have my love, the dear ones who are old now.
Yiskidor, all men and women are my brothers and sisters now.
Yiskidor, how I love men, now that I have dared
to look in their eyes
and stand my ground as the energies connect.
Yiskidor, if men would reach out and hold each other
they would know we are all brothers.
Yiskidor, I am my father's son, God help me.
Yiskidor, I am my father's son, the heir
to the mess he couldn't solve.
Yiskidor, thank God I am my mother's son too
for what she gave me
is what I survived by.
I cry Mamma, and am healed.
Yiskidor, I am my father's son.
Even if I can't stand it, still
I am.

SHARKS

Especially at evening
everyone knows the sharks come in
when the sun makes puddles of blood on the sea
and the shadows darken.

It is then, as night comes on
the sharks of deep water
approach the shore
and beware, beware, the late swimmer.

from NEW AND SELECTED POEMS (1987)

TRIAD

A temple sculpture: Two Warriors in Combat.
Down between their knees, a female,
with the prick of one of them up her cunt
and, at the same time, bending over backwards
to take the other's cock in her mouth —
while the men cross swords over her.

Even confronting each other with sharp steel,
according to this ancient mystery
something tender bridges them,
a goddess joining the warriors in her body —
for she has to be a goddess
and this is obviously her function.
But is she consoling, neutralizing,
trying to bring peace about,
or delivering the charge
that sets their swords a-clashing?

Or do they only appear to fight
to deny the sexual connection below?
But no one seems to be hiding anything —
it's open as a diagram, illustrative,
rather than a daisy chain like The Three Graces.

When we say men are joined in battle
do we too mean like this,
opposition at one pole, concord at the other,
and in the contest both at once?
Beyond the fierce, worldly display,
the glitter of rivalry, the squiring of women —
a secret brotherhood?

And even against their will,
create this goddess out of a deeper need.

It's within a female principle men unite.

TWO SONGS

How hard I tried to be hard,
        to be arrogant and strong
like all those men I admired
        to whom I could never belong.

But, ah, friend, life is a breaker of backs
and from the dark balcony, on a movie screen in my head
I look at the youth I was then
who wouldn't be kissed and who wouldn't kiss,
and had not even begun to face his worthlessness,

and scorning as sissy all softness
as the years went rushing by,
crushed the longings of my sentimental heart.

                    ◄ • ►

If today I am haggard and old
I've got no right to complain —
all through the years I was told
that I looked much younger than
I had any right to be.
I heard it again and again
but it meant less than nothing to me.
The unhappy youth I was then
in the dark pit of distress
couldn't take advantage of
that much-praised youthfulness
or any of the generous
(it now seems) offers of love —
none of that meant a thing.

And what also has to be faced
is if youth was a waste
it wasn't fate's but my own doing.

SHY GUY

Such a dear fellow, such a shy one,
doing his job but never praised for it,
dug at, scratched, and harshly wiped,
either ignored in public
or joked about.
Put yourself in his place:
How do you feel
when somebody calls you an asshole?

The face gets endless care and beautifying,
and though he's dying to be glamorous too,
nobody uses makeup on him.
The hair is brushed and dressed,
the hands caressed,

the eyes looked deeply into,
and even the cunt . . . a man I know
claims he can stare at a cunt for hours—
but who wants to gaze up an asshole?

Frustrated in his longings
for, if not public recognition,
at least appreciation, do you blame him,
ordered to squeeze himself tight
and not let out a peep for hours,
for dropping a loud one
in the middle of a cocktail party
or your big romantic moment?

We take his cooperation for granted,
and then it's all his fault, when sore with piles
or sullen in constipation,
he soon learns he gets plenty of attention,

though not the kind he craves:
we throw up our hands and submit him
to the harsh spotlights of medical procedures
or worse, the surgical amphitheatre,

never imagining what's wrong is us,
for identifying him with the shit
he so elegantly expels.

Categories I: Nurses and Patients

If we divide the world into nurses and patients
I am a born nurse
and you, a born patient.

I am in a passion of taking care of you
and you demand constant, unremitting attention —
we found each other.

Your ailments increase in scope and complexity
as I struggle to keep you well,
finding cures, solutions to your problems.

Your needs are a mountain
and I am an ant
moving it grain by grain —
I daren't stop for a moment.

How to keep you alive, my darling,
when life seems to have cheated you,
rewarding you only with troubles galore.

In your view, that is somehow all my fault.
I am supposed to make it up to you,
for you see me as one of the lucky ones,
who have been given everything in life —
looks, lovers, success, and luck.

My luck, angel, is only to have found you,
the large, demanding child I adore,
the child of the world I worship,
the child of myself I care for, my sweet pain.

The more I give, the more you demand—
I can never do enough, I know. Failure, failure.
Still, I am grateful to have found
a way to be useful in life: thank you
for that supreme gift.
To me you are a radiant being
I am honored to serve.

Nurse has found the perfect patient,
patient the perfect nurse,
and care will be unrelenting.

Both parties agree there will be no cure.

MIRROR SONG

It's in the bathroom that I loudly groan
    over my incandescent foolishness —

when I think of what I've said and done,
especially tonight at the dinner table. . . .
    O why did I have to blab like that
among those grown-up people?

You are a jerk and never will be other,
and right thou art to know thy estimate:
    It's written all over your silly face,

and therefore, you may well invoke
    the eternal fraternal principle,
a cry resounding down the ages

      to Gods and man alike,
      from Job to Christ-on-the-Cross to you:

O Brother!

CATEGORIES II: COWS AND BULLS

You can always spot a bull—
when one comes into the room
the cows flock round.

It is easy to spot two bulls—
they lock horns on sight.

It has nothing to do with gender.
Psychiatrists are wrong to encourage
every man to be the bull
and the wife the family cow
when often it's the other way—
there's no changing essences.

Raised to think they're bulls
men inside are lowing love me,
and women forced to be fluffy are born to be boss,
engendering feminist rage—okay,
bellow in protest, but if you don't
simply start being the bull you are,
sister, you're just rattling your chains.

Every couple must work out for themselves
who's bull and who's cow—
what a relief, anyhow,
not to have to play-act bull or cow,
and if you're a cow, it saves years of misery to know
not to expect from another cow
love's fireworks, though fooling around's okay
while waiting for the bull—
Don't worry, there'll be no doubt
when the real thing comes along.

As the bull said to the zebra at the zoo
    who asked him what he did,
"Take off those striped pajamas, kid,
    and I'll show you what I do."

Once you've been stranded in desert
you love all wetness—
the splashing of fountains at sundown in dusty plazas,
even the banal dribble of faucets,
become total pleasure.

When your ramshackle bus breaks down on a remote plain
you wait and wait, squatting in its shadow
with the robed and veiled, the more patient ones than you.
You try to take comfort from
the barren sweep of mountain ahead
and the nomad encampment visible on a far slope, as stony as
                this one.
The ear is assailed by a buzz of insects,
perhaps around a patch of stiff, staring-eyed sunflowers
rattled by gusts.
Something grew them there, surely,
but long ago.

No water is wet enough
to irrigate the thirst that grows here now,
though Pepsi-Cola, if there was any, would be ambrosia.
But, the ancients say,
better not drink in heat of day—wait for sundown.
Still, the imagination goes desolate,
pictures thirst-crazed lost staggerers
after illusory lakes on false horizons.

Hours, or is it days, of this,
and when you can't stand it anymore, the first change occurs,
like a shift in bedrock, a settling of the floor—
you accept being stuck there.
One place is as good as another, so why not here?

Someone begins playing a wild jangle of music
and there is even a breeze.

It is then that rescue comes, a truck
crowded with molten-eyed men in rakish turbans,
and you climb up onto piles of bags in back
full of some scratchy harvest of wool or wheat,
and after an hour of bumping over a stony track
the mud walls greet you of an oasis town
where intense gardens enclose pomegranate trees
at once in fruit and flower.

And finally in a caravanserai-hotel
where the men settle down cross-legged with pots of tea
on rug-draped divans in the gloom
comes the ultimate, soul-drenching blessing in the desert world,
the world of the ancestors, of the old power:

In your room you strip off dust-caked clothes
down to tender skin, pores open to everything now,
and turn on the shower.

To Love

Away from home on a tour in the West
I worried about you constantly, my dearest,
until I had a dream one night where you
were a large plant I was chopping down with a shovel:
first I slashed off your feet
and then battered your head in, that head
that has already been attacked
by scalpel, drill, and saw,
and is always blindly bumping things,
making my heart ache.

I woke in a sweat of course
but after the shock wore away that I
could do such a thing to you, my angel, even in a dream,
I saw how absolutely necessary it was—
your needs had pursued me across a continent
and this was the only way of getting free, of renouncing
even for a week the relentless care of you,
the concern of my days and nights: how to keep you,
an exotic, delicate plant, alive in an arctic clime—
though in my dream, I must admit,
you were a vigorous weed, towering over me.

And then, my leafy, my green one,
whom I water daily and put in the sun,
after chopping you down and shoveling you away
I could leave you in God's hands—
and loving you not the less for being free,
went almost light-hearted on with my journey.

THE CRIER

As much as I'd like to be
a jolly, fat old man,
skinny I remain
no matter what I eat,

and jolly I'll never become—
though I perfectly understand
the reasons for that, the same
as prevent me from getting fat.

But if I go on living,
unlikely as it seems
with signs of doom in my hand
and symptoms multiplying,

I can't think of anything
that I would rather do
than spend my old age crying—
if they allow me to.

Printed October 1992 in Santa Barbara & Ann
Arbor for the Black Sparrow Press by Mackintosh
Typography & Edwards Brothers Inc. Text set in
Bembo by Words Worth. Design by Barbara Martin.
This edition is published in paper wrappers;
there are 200 hardcover trade copies;
125 hardcover copies have been numbered & signed
by the author; & 26 copies handbound in boards
by Earle Gray are lettered & signed by the author.

EDWARD FIELD was born June 7, 1924 in Brooklyn, New York, and grew up on Long Island, where he played cello in the Field Family Trio over radio station WGBB. During World War II he flew 25 missions over Europe. After a short time at New York University on the GI Bill, he returned to Europe where he began writing seriously—the details can be found in the poem "Bio"—and his poems started appearing in literary magazines, from *Botteghe Oscure, Evergreen Review,* and *The New York Review of Books* to *Wormwood Review, Exquisite Corpse,* and *American Poetry Review.* His first book, *Stand Up, Friend, With Me,* won the Lamont Award in 1962, followed by a Guggenheim Fellowship, the Prix de Rome, and the Shelley Memorial Award. He has given readings at the Library of Congress and at universities all over the country, and has taught workshops at the Poetry Center—YMHA, Sarah Lawrence and other colleges.

Besides collections of poetry, which include an illustrated book of his movie poems, he has edited anthologies of modern poetry and wrote the narration for the documentary film, *To Be Alive,* which won an Academy Award. He collaborates on fiction with Neil Derrick, under the pseudonym of Bruce Elliot. He is also the editor of *The Alfred Chester Newsletter,* and has prepared several volumes of Chester's work for Black Sparrow Press. He lives in New York, but spends as much time as he can in foreign places.